W9-COY-539

DIMENSIONS FOR HAPPENING

Lois Horton Young

dimensions
for
happening

Judson Press
Valley Forge

DIMENSIONS FOR HAPPENING

International Standard Book No. 0-8170-0506-4
Library of Congress Catalog Card No. 76-144081

Printed in the U.S.A.

To Andy for whom art has opened
worlds,
with seeking love

CONTENTS

INTRODUCTION

Dimensions for Happening is an invitation to a new teaching-learning adventure which may be described as the Art-Response Experience. In this experience, individuals are encouraged to use art as a means of expressing their response to the Bible.

The approach to sharing and discovering the Christian faith that is delineated in the suggestions and experiments on the following pages is based on the assumptions that:

1. God can and does speak through the Bible when we hear it read simply, directly, expressively, and that he may be more clearly heard when an atmosphere for listening is created.

2. The Bible has significance for the present condition of the person who hears it, and it is heard by each person in the light of all he is and of his life situation at the moment of hearing, as well as in the light of his potential for becoming through the grace of God.

3. All persons are capable of continuous nonverbal response, which is an outflowing of thought and emotion, and which can be channeled through the use of materials available in their hands.

The Art-Response Experience Unrolls in This Way:
An atmosphere is created to develop each person's readiness for hearing and responding to God who speaks through the Bible.

Opportunity is provided for listening to the reading of the Bible while art media are ready in hand so that each individual may spontaneously and continuously respond to what he is hearing.

After the reading and the nonverbal response is complete,

9

a period of sharing through speaking, hearing one another, and seeing adds further depth, confrontation, and involvement.

This gives us several simultaneous dimensions to be brought into focus as we move into and through such a teaching-learning adventure; dimensions in terms of the Bible, of art, and of personal growth.

The Art-Response Experience Covers Many Age Levels and Situations.

The Art-Response Experience has prime effectiveness when used with youth or adults in a series of several sessions. However, it is very useful in and adds new zest to a number of other situations in which there is teaching-learning.

It offers many possibilities for exciting experiences for the elementary-aged child.

It can be used within a family or with a group where several age levels are represented, for each person is free to respond nonverbally to meanings that come to him in terms with which he is comfortable.

It offers an exciting teaching-learning method for a short series of sessions or for a course continuing for many weeks.

It may be appropriated in part to provide a fresh approach as an experience utilizing all the time available within one setting or session.

It may even be adapted for use as part of a session.

Even limited application of this teaching-learning experience may provide fresh insights, growing understanding, and spontaneous joy.

The Art-Response Experience provides incentives for:

EXPLORING TOGETHER. Whenever a group enters into an experience with art response, whether for a single session or over a series of *meet*-ings, there can well be a mood of expectancy, innovation, and experimentation. Expect that God will reveal himself. Be flexible and free to innovate. Know that nothing is cut-and-dried and predictable; there are too many variable factors and we cannot know how God will work.

INVOLVING INDIVIDUALS. The approach provides for the involvement of each individual with the personal and social messages of the Bible.

He is involved with creativity and self-expression.

He is involved with personal responsibility for the success of the experience for himself and for others.

HELPING GROWING PERSONS TO MATURE. The approach is addressed to growing persons. At the same time, it assumes that persons have gained some maturity, or are willing to strive for growth. To this end, participants must agree to some disciplines without which a great deal turns out to be lost motion or simply running around in circles. The art-response approach acknowledges the worth of each person, and recognizes that every person has something to contribute, that nobody has a monopoly on ideas and insights, and that each individual's response gives some impetus to the whole experience and moves it in a direction which means growth for all. Persons need to reach for growing and changing wherever changing means finding one's self and finding God.

LOOKING TO GOD AS TEACHER. The art-response acknowledges the presence of God to teach and guide us. The leader does not come with ideas to expound or explain, with information to "tell," with content to "get across." The students do not come with "beefs" to spout, "hangups" to hang or pet peeves to pout over. Leaders are learners and students are teachers when all come to open their minds to God and hear him speak. He then can, and DOES.

The heart of the Art-Response Experience consists of
THREE DISCIPLINES. To these each teacher-learner must agree:

1. I shall open my mind to God.
2. I shall seek to concentrate and project myself into the experience.
3. I shall respect the ideas of others.

These can be restated or adapted as desired, but the essential core of each should be maintained intact. They can be shaped, lettered, presented, and worded as you will, but should find a place on the wall to be reminders at each session. The forms on this page are merely suggestive.

1. I SHALL
open
my mind
TO
GOD
I SHALL REACH for
I SHALL
PRAY

2. I SHALL seek to CONCENTRATE
I SHALL PROJECT MYSELF INTO THE MOOD & SPIRIT OF THE EXPERIENCE

3. I SHALL respect and reverence THE IDEAS OF OTHERS
I SHALL NOT
be judgmental of
or laugh at
THEM

The Art-Response Experience is multidimensional.

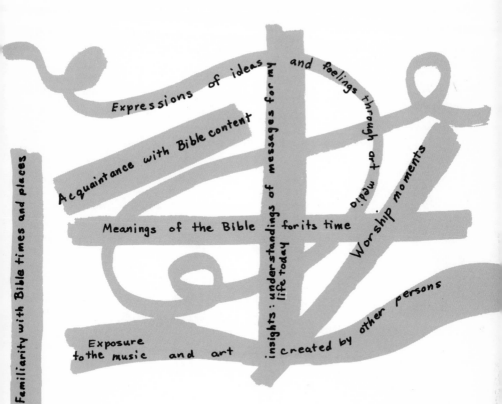

Expressions of ideas and feelings through art media

Acquaintance with Bible content

insights: understandings of messages for my life today

Worship moments

Familiarity with Bible times and places

Meanings of the Bible for its time

Exposure to the music and art created by other persons

Each of the dimensions in the scheme above adds richness and character to the experience of every person in a group. Each of these dimensions calls for planning, innovation, prayer, and opening the mind and heart to God's guidance as it comes in many ways, in many places, at any moment, through any person or thing.

As members of the group contribute elements of these dimensions to the experience of all, the perspective of interpersonal relationships and the pervading sense of God's presence deepen every dimension.

MULTIDIMENSIONS

13

To put it still another way:
God reaches for man
    through the words of the Bible;
    through the atmosphere of worship, of music, of art, of
        meditation which is created for his speaking;
    through the persons who are a part of the group.

Man reaches for God
    through thinking of him;
    through responding to his Book by means of creative art
        media;
    through conscious awareness that he may speak at any
        moment in any way.

Man reaches for man
    through recording impressions and sharing these impres-
        sions and insights;
    through stretching toward understanding and appreciat-
        ing the uniqueness of each person in the group.

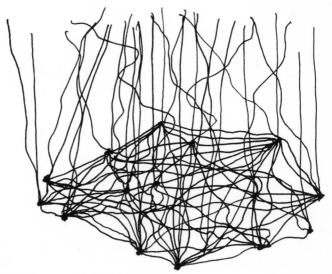

In a happening, relationships come alive.
There is a mysterious plus factor quite beyond our understanding.
In quietness, we hear God as we have not heard him before.
And we hear one another in new ways.

Part 1
CONSIDERING DIMENSIONS

Let us now begin to examine the aspects of the art-response approach which relate to the Bible. There are relationships between past and present, between ideas and the person in the group, between things and the person, between God and the person. They may be viewed as goals before they happen, and as outcomes after they happen. Measuring the extent to which each happens could serve as a way of evaluating the experience. Each calls for its own particular form of concrete planning in order to make it as rich, as meaningful, as inviting, as effective as possible.

• *The Reading of the Bible.* Three questions flash into mind: What shall be read? How shall it be read? When shall it be read? Consideration of these questions offers a good starting point for planning an experience for a group.

What shall be read?

The choice of passages to be included may become the organizing principle of an art-response experience. A number of possibilities are open here. Some of the following suggestions may apply also if a single session is to be planned rather than a series of sessions.

Passages may be chosen by *expressed group interest.* If this is the criterion for selection, some opportunity will need to be given for persons to indicate their interests. Perhaps the simplest way of doing this is to provide group members with a form to be completed and returned to the planner.[1] While all the passages indicated as preferences probably will be impossible, choices can be made to include a number of them, and a sequence can be

[1] See Appendix: Profiles in Participation.

determined by setting selections in order and tentatively allotting a block of time to each over the period of weeks that are available. This plan should be kept flexible, for different timing may develop once the plan is in progress.

Passages may be chosen by *book,* one book providing the basic content for one course, or two or more shorter books may be used. In general, material that is primarily narrative can be covered in a shorter length of time: moving rapidly and less analytically provides cleaner, clearer impacts and tends to command better attention to content and more intensive responses from members of the group. More abstract or "meaty" material will need to be read at a more leisurely pace, or read repeatedly to allow more time for meditation and response. The type of material being used and the art medium in which the group is responding has an important relationship to the pace chosen for reading.

Passages may be chosen by their relationship to a *central theme,* such as the mission of the church, the parables of Jesus, Christian conscience, social justice, God the Creator, or any other major idea to which portions of the Bible speak. If this is the criterion for selection, all material in a given course should be related to the central theme chosen, and each portion should have sufficient volume to provide the basis for at least a block of time in which a satisfying art response can develop without the interruption of transitions.

Passages may be chosen by their historical context. An example of this would be the biography of David and the Psalms attributed to him.

If the art-response method is being used to enrich an experience with an *already-established curriculum course,* the biblical material listed in the course will provide the basis for selection of passages to be used.

In any case, important considerations in the choice of passages will be the needs of the persons involved — the age group, for example — and the position of the course in the church's general curriculum of Christian education.

Since the primary purpose of reading is communication, *recent translations of the Bible* should be used. These speak to our time with particular freshness and reflect ideas that are closer to the original meanings and less distorted by the evolution of our present language from the language of the past. The version selected should be used throughout any given course, whether the particular version is Moffatt, Phillips, the New English Bible, the Revised Standard Version, or Good News for Modern Man.

Where the art-response method is new to all or some persons of a group, *a sampling session* should be provided before beginning on the main thrust of the course. This sampling session should provide opportunity to hear and respond to a short passage set in a context of introduction to the stance and procedures of the course.[2] This enables participants to gain some momentum and freedom to "find their sea legs." The passage chosen for this sampling need not be related to the passages to be used in the balance of the course, but should whet everyone's appetite for participation.

How shall the Bible be read?

One reader who is able to vary his pace, expression, pitch, tone, and emphasis should be chosen to do the reading for the first several sessions. The "teacher" of the course may be qualified for this role, and probably in most cases should be the reader. In general, students should not be asked to take over the reading but should be able to use their time in responding to the reading. Guest readers may be used, or at times a reading prerecorded on tape could be substituted. This offers variety and introduces an element of surprise which adds to the richness of the experience.

There should be no noises or distractions which would prevent the reading from being clearly heard. No conversation whatever between any persons in the room should be permitted while the reading is in progress or until it is completed for the day. The reason for this is that only as each person is granted his right to hear the Bible read and is allowed freedom to respond in art forms without the interjection of the ideas of other persons, is his response truly of his own self.

Agreeing to the Three Disciplines (see Introduction) requires

---

[2] See section on *Pencil,* The Art Dimension, page 25.

participants to channel their expressed response to a situation into the form designated for that particular block of time. This means that during the reading of the Bible no verbal response is appropriate; but all energy is channeled into the art response. This absence of conversation respects the right of each person to respond to the words of the Bible, to the Spirit of God, without having others impose ideas that distract from the main thrust of the experience.

Innovations utilizing sound can provide for transitions that do not require comment from the reader, or can enhance the reading itself. The exclusion of *distracting* sound does not rule out *contributing* sound.

On occasion sound may be planned to heighten the effect of the reading. Three examples, the first two from the reading of psalms, may serve to illustrate the point.

On a morning in which Psalm 150 was the focus of our art-response experience, the psalm was read several times at different paces and with different pauses and emphases. One reading was done with a background of a Bach Concerto; this was followed by another reading with appropriate pauses so that the words and phrases were paced with the music.

A tape of nature sounds — storm, waves, wind in the trees, and bird songs — was developed to accompany Psalm 104. A tape recording of the sounds of waves could serve as background for the reading of Exodus 14 and 15 which tell of the people of God being led through the Red Sea.

The salient point to keep in mind here is that the character and volume of any accompanying sounds must enhance the text being read, not distract from it. Occasional rather than continuous use of any supplementary sound is effective. Sound must not become a gimmick.

Reference has been made to providing for transitions in ways which will not mar the continuity of an experience and will not break a train of thought or the flow of a response. Let us illustrate what is meant.

In an experience with Isaiah 41, in which each paragraph was to occupy one space in a projected paper folder, the leader held a brace of five small bells from Palestine. In the pause following each paragraph, the gently rung bells indicated that a paragraph had been completed, and that the student should move to the next space to respond to the new paragraph that was beginning. (See Part 3: Showcase of Ideas, section 17.)

As groups work with the experience of art response to Bible reading, new ideas will develop for effective ways to read.

When shall the Bible be read?

The major block of time in each session is to be devoted to reading the Bible to the group while the members respond through using art media.

The length of the Reading and Response period (see third section of Part 2) can vary somewhat, depending on the age group to whom the experience is being offered and the intensity of the group's interest. The total length of time available for each session will be a factor. The leader will find a difference in the mood of the group from session to session and will become sensitive to this. He will discover that some sessions move briskly and others are marked by a leisurely, meditative mood. Sometimes a spirit pervades the Saturation Sally (see Part 2) which says clearly, "Wait, we are already on holy ground." At other times you will come to know when it is "right" to get on to the reading.

One role of the leader is to guard against getting carried away so that the time for reading is cut down, or so that inadequate time is left to bring the session to a meaningful conclusion (see Part 2: The Windup) through sharing responses and worship moments.

No strict time schedule will be established, and there can be much flexibility, but always the major block of time should be kept intact for the Bible reading and art response. Exception to this will be adapting this teaching-learning procedure to enrich an already-planned curriculum course, in which case the Bible reading will be allotted a much smaller time segment of the session.

• *Enriching Our Understanding of the Bible.* To offer fresh invitations for learning about Bible life and times is one of the goals of the art-response approach. As these invitations are accepted and learning takes place, students gain new dimensions for understanding the ideas of the Bible and can therefore respond in a more enlightened and vigorous way.

True, these are *invitations to* not *injections of* learning, and

19

there will be wide differences in both the volume and kinds of appropriation by the individual students. The idea is to provide a variety of materials and situations for learning, and to provide for each person both the time and the setting conducive to choosing what has the strongest interest for him. What kinds of materials may be offered, and where and when may they be made available?

What materials will invite to enrichment of Bible background?

Through displaying materials selectively on the walls, ceilings, table and floor surfaces of the room, and also on such open space as windows, windowsills, shelves, and the top of a cabinet or piano, students may be invited to examine resources which appeal to them. This does not mean the room becomes a clutter, or that students should be overwhelmed by an extensive spread of distractions. It does mean that the leader will plan carefully both the content of resources and the manner in which they are displayed. Not only will what is offered be varied and continually changing, but it will be relevant to the Bible passages being read in the sessions; and members of the group will be encouraged to contribute findings of their own to what is available to all.

Innovation can make all of this an exciting experience, and free both the appearance and content of the session from the drabness and routine of the usual presentations. It is amazing what love can devise. And behind what is obvious, back of the gathering and displaying of resources, is the leader's love for each person and the drive to inveigle him into discovering how rich, how relevant, how intriguing the Bible really is. Our motivation is not the desire to be different for the sake of differentness or sensationalism, but rather the willingness to be different for the sake of gaining thoughtful attention or calling to discovery.

You may want to choose certain areas of the room where materials for Bible enrichment will be featured.[3] A shelf can serve to display books on Bible life and times, a Bible dictionary, a Bible atlas, and other reference works in which students can look up items of special interest. Here too may be placed a few

[3] See Part 4: Tools for Planning for suggested Bible background and enrichment materials.

selected books especially related to the course which can be borrowed for home reading.

Charts, maps, and flat pictures chosen with discrimination may occupy a bulletin board area. One teacher used a low ceiling to display a large map. Does this suggest new possibilities? A table may be used for realia (*real* objects significant to text) and a slide projector may be set up for students to use at will. Single slides correlated with biblical material for the session may be projected against a screen which is backed to the light so that viewing is clear. If you have access to an overhead projector, use it occasionally to display a picture or resource piece on a wall for wider viewing to add interest.

When may Bible background materials be used?

We have mentioned the possibility that some student may become sufficiently interested in a subject or question related to the biblical material being read during the sessions to want to borrow for *home use* some of the attractive materials made available for enrichment reading. The skilled leader will find occasion for stimulating interest and suggesting something especially likely to hold the attention of a particular person. This must be, needless to say, in the area of an invitation, not an assignment or suggestion with accompanying pressure.

As the group is gathering at the *beginning of the session,* some persons may want to arrange or examine new exhibits of Bible-related material while others distribute art materials to be used for the day.

These two uses of enrichment materials just mentioned are very well known to all who have had previous teaching experience: namely, the assignment of enrichment material for home study, and the opportunity for persons to browse among books and exhibits when they first arrive in the classroom. But the time uniquely provided in the art-response experience is the Saturation Sally which you will find described in detail in Part 2: Projecting a Session. Directly preceding the Bible reading and art response, this period is designed to give each person a time for exploration, meditation, preparation, and creation of a mood of receptiveness for listening and responding to what God will say through the Book. While this is a period of following individual leads, and persons may choose to use their time for contemporary art or other kinds of viewing or reading material, Bible enrichment should always be in the mind of the person arranging for the music, art objects, and books to be offered at any session.

A few specific illustrations may serve to clarify this point. For the session in which a group was to work with the Shepherd Psalm, all the material laid out for the Saturation Sally was chosen for the purpose of setting a mood of familiarity with shepherd life. On a large table (a Ping-Pong table with net removed is an ideal size) were placed in random arrangement: pictures of shepherds and sheep; books with markers at articles and at pictures about shepherds; magazines open at shepherd-related material (a *National Geographic* and an *Aramco World*); copies of art masterpieces in which a shepherd's care is the theme, as Picasso's "Le Bergere"; a model of a sheepfold; a doll dressed in shepherd costume; a handful of fleece; toy lambs and sheep of various sorts. The music used as listening atmosphere for this period was "He Shall Feed His Flock" from Handel's *Messiah*.

As the group moved silently about, studying or picking up materials from the table, or taking a chosen book to a chair, or standing in silent contemplation, a feeling of stillness began to pervade the room. It was a stillness that went deep inside each one, and made all ready for the presence of God.

When we were "doing" the story of Joseph, specific biblical resource materials used included pictures to enrich concepts of the Egypt of Joseph's time, traveling by camel, and a picture or two from the picture file which illustrated some event in the life of Joseph. Of course, materials not directly related to biblical times were used also.

Take-home-and-keep pieces offer another way and time for growing in understanding the Bible. The leader may provide for each student a copy of material he believes might have value in enlarging understanding of Bible content.

Such material might include an outline of a book or section of a book that has been read, a page with definitions of terms, a sheet of thumbnail sketches of major characters, notes about customs or places, or summaries of one sort or another. Some examples will be found in Part 4: Tools for Planning. The use of these resources should be discreet and limited. In some cases the pages might be embellished with art work by a member of the class or they might be developed entirely by a student who finds such a project appealing. If placed in each student's folder, envelope, or portfolio containing his art work, these selected materials help to serve him as a record and reminder of a personal and group experience with the Bible.

The biblical dimension is the prime dimension in the art-response method. No other kind of reading can be substituted for it. No other material is on a par with it for emphasis or focus of attention. No other content offers comparable intrigue or should compete for its priority.

Belief in this fact provided the rationale for the creation of this educational approach: namely, that through the Bible God speaks to the need and condition of man in a singular way. Therefore, as the person is exposed to hearing the Bible, God can speak to him and bring his life to fullness through the unique God-man relationship, thereby changing man's relationship, to himself, to the world around him, and to other persons in his family and in his community.

Art is another dimension in which there is "happening" as a group learns together through the Art-Response Experience. This occurs in two respects: in the creation of art and in the appreciation of art. Let us look closely at each of these.

• *Creating Art Forms in Response to Hearing the Bible.* The joy of creating through art forms gains momentum with practice. In an atmosphere where mind and feelings are yielded to the greatness of biblical exposure, the self-consciousness which hampers expression of the impulse to respond diminishes and self-assurance grows. Freedom to do what you feel begins to release the potential response of each person. Self-discovery happens as each individual finds that what he produces through his art says something no one else can say and in a way no one else can say it. The spark of desire to respond, which exists in every person, is nourished and allowed to grow.

Referring to the Three Disciplines, agreement to which is prerequisite to participation in the art-response experience, you will see that obviously an important tenet on which rests the success of the art-response approach is the respect of each person for

THE ART DIMENSION

23

the worth of each other person in the group. This fosters openness, sincerity, and freedom in creating art forms.

ART MEDIA AND TECHNIQUES

To respond with freedom and joy is an objective of this teaching-learning method; to produce great art, or any other kind of art for that matter, is not an objective. What results in art forms is a by-product and not a goal. There is no emphasis therefore on developing or perfecting art techniques, and any skills or talents gained through experience in an art-response course are quite incidental. The processes of using the various media are not of importance beyond their freeing of the person's response. This limits both the choice of media and the suggested techniques to what is effective in terms of carrying forward the purposes of the study.

The following may be considered as criteria for the selection of art materials and techniques:

They must be sufficiently inexpensive to be plentiful.

They must be simple enough to be used easily by any person who has never used them before.

They must be capable of recording an individual's response quickly and not call for painstaking execution.

Seldom will the art reflect a totality except that "the total is the sum of its parts." For the kind of response that is called forth will be a series of expressed reactions to the successive small facets of an unfolding Bible passage. In the art-response experience when involvement becomes studied or premeditated, there is a risk of losing spontaneity.

This does not say that any person who is especially interested in art will be discouraged from spending additional time outside of group sessions on his work should he wish to do so. And it does not limit a group which has had previous experience in the art-response method from developing innovations or more sophisticated procedures of its own. In fact, such a group may even wish to establish extra sessions for work as the members become really absorbed in what they are doing. That is fine if the initiative comes from the group, not from the leader.

Let us look at some of the media which lend themselves best to the art-response experience, and offer a few ideas for the effective use of each.

24

Pencil. This is a good introductory medium. It is small, hard, reassuring, and private, and paper strips or rectangles on which the pencil is used can be small enough to give beginners a sense of freedom from being observed by other persons. Actually they will discover that each person is much too absorbed in what he himself is doing to have time or interest in watching someone else work while the period of Bible reading is in progress. But as he makes his first ventures, better than reassurance from the leader will be his own security with the familiar pencil and his own discovery that he can respond easily. Pencils of a different size may be used for a second experience.

Felt-tip marker. Characterized by intense color of varied hues, felt-tip markers are quick drying, versatile, permanent, and lend themselves to rapid execution of an idea. For the felt-tip marker, more effective than a rectangular piece of paper and more inviting to free response is a strip of newsprint six inches wide and 24 inches long. An ample supply of these and of felt-tip markers can be within easy reach of every person before the work begins, and the paper strips can be assembled in sequence in many ways when the session ends. They can be used vertically or horizontally, but for practical reasons, one direction or the other should be established as the procedure for everyone during a current project.

This form of response is especially good for narrative books, such as Acts, Ruth, or Nehemiah. For these a vertical use, working from top to bottom, is recommended. When the passage being read is long, the strips can be folded into sections, using a section for each paragraph; in this case left to right procedure is suggested.

This method may be referred to as "felt-tip marker recordings" or "droodles," as you choose — or the group may want to suggest its own terminology.

Chalk. Soft and easy to blend, chalk fills surfaces rapidly and easily produces striking effects. Rough papers like bogus or brown wrapping paper work well with this medium. There may be some problems in using chalk but these can be handled by providing what is needed to deal with them. Chalk can be messy and some people do not like the feel of it on their hands. For easier cleanup, cover tables with newspapers and place shallow boxes (such as hosiery boxes) where chalk can be shared with another person, kept easily available and, when the session is over, stored quickly simply by stacking boxes. Ideally, students should be dressed informally, or some coverup may be available. Damp sponges should be at hand for wetting paper or wiping fingers, and finished work may be sprayed with a plastic spray fixative or hair spray to set the color.

Schnitzen (Cut-and-Paste). This medium has several advantages and will become a favorite when a group grows accustomed to it. Schnitzen offers a choice of textures, patterns, and colors; it gives variety in effects; it offers a new tool and motion; it allows for individual effort but can be used in a collective response as well.

One method of offering this material is to provide boxes of assorted papers about 5 x 5" from which each student can select a pile of those pieces with which he wishes to work. The papers can be lined, plain, patterned, of any weight or color; everything from ad sections of newspapers to wallpaper to origami or construction paper is usable. Members of the group will enjoy bringing in contributions to the stockpile (one teenager sponge printed and washed with watercolor a stack of papers to contribute for group use).

Each student begins with a pile of paper in front of him and a pair of scissors in hand. As the reading proceeds he cuts forms from one paper after another, piling them in order as completed. When the reading is finished, these may be pasted to a background as desired.[4]

Clay. Salt-flour clay (see page 84 for recipe) is recommended because it can be quite colorful, is clean and easy to use, and can be ornamented with colored fragments of glass, eggshells, chips or stones and become a mosaic. The usefulness of clay is limited because it requires more time to form a response. It is suitable, however, when a single form is acceptable as a response to a whole passage. To give adequate time to respond and to deepen impressions, the passage may be reread after a short interlude of silence, or a recording may offer added time for work and meditation.

Crayons. Crayons obviously meet the criteria suggested for choosing material, but we mention them here with some hesitancy for two reasons. First, they are so common to the average

[4] See accounts of specific experiences on pages 49, and 70 (#38).

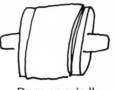

Drum on spindle

Continuous roll   Stapled into booklet

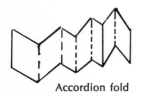

Accordion fold

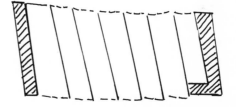

Winding board (turn to
view continuous sequence)

Some suggestions for assembling and for viewing the continuous recordings reproduced as felt-tip marker droodles:

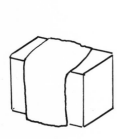

Turning box

Double roller frame

Curved fanfold

person that the freshness of a new experience may be limited because his approach has been conditioned by all the associations and feelings he has had with crayons in the past. And second, crayons are the easiest answer for any leader to provide: "Ah! Crayons!" and we latch onto the idea and get no farther.

The art-response experience should be one of new venture and daring; thus if this medium is offered, provide a rich assortment of colors and some innovative work surfaces varying in shapes and types of paper. A number of processes in which crayons are used can be exciting. (See pages 54 and 65, #20 and #21.)

These limited suggestions for the use of basic art media offer a good variety for any course of several weeks, and provide a strong comfortable ground for a leader who is beginning to use the art-response teaching-learning method.

As students and teachers work with the art-response experience, they will discover other media and other techniques adapted to the objectives. The possibilities are legion, but the suggestions just given will serve as a good beginning and easily will carry a group through twelve to eighteen sessions. Having gained a feel for the method and developed a drive to experiment with other materials in other ways, you can go on from there. Further suggestions may be found in the balance of the book, especially in Part 3: Showcase of Ideas, and in the Bibliography and the Recipes sections. The only point to remember is to test proposed media and techniques against the criteria for selection in the light of the goals of the course. It is a good idea to practice-use or test privately in advance what you plan to offer the group to make certain your plans are completely workable.

FINISHED ART SPEAKS

Of great value in giving new insights to each of us is the opportunity to look at the ways members of the group have responded to a biblical passage and to hear some of the thoughts and feelings they had as they were working.

Therefore in each session, we look forward to the time set apart when the Bible reading is ended and students share and tell about what they have done. Some of the high moments of the course will come as persons reveal the thinking that went into their work, and each one finds new meaning in the fresh insights that have come to someone else. (See Sharing and Analysis in Part 2.) It is surprising how vividly these will stay with you as you go out from the group.

• *Art Dimensions Contributed from Other Sources.* There is a place in the art-response experience for exposure to works by persons not in the group whose skills in creating art forms can give impetus to our own efforts. Some of these works are in the field of music, some in the fine arts. Some are the art of old masters, some the expression of contemporary life.

In any case, listening and looking can begin to create in us some momentum and can contribute to our receptivity. This dimension is primarily associated with the Saturation Sally (see Saturation Sally in Part 2), in which there is an attempt to open the mind to impressions and to establish a readiness to appropriate what is meaningful to us.

Music Listening

There is a wealth of recordings available for borrowing, from your library or from individuals, and these can be chosen not only with a view to correlation with the mood of the Bible passages of the day, but with some attention to the type of music which will probably call forth the greatest response from the particular group with which it is being used. Since tastes in music differ, some variety in kind has merit, and a choice which includes modern as well as traditional composers can broaden horizons of appreciation. However, the music should not become the focus of attention but rather be blended in the atmosphere which sensitizes the spirit and contributes to receptivity. For this reason recordings must usually be without words, or in words of an unfamiliar language (Latin, French, Hebrew, German), must be controlled in volume, and must not be dramatic in expression. This also rules out live music, which is too visual. (There are additional comments on music in the section entitled "Hearing," Saturation Sally, Part 2.)

An exception to this would be a hymn, song, or instrumental music closely related to the biblical material read in the session, in which case such music would probably be used at the beginning or end of the hour. This use would usually be preplanned. (See list or recordings in Part 4: Tools for Planning.)

From the moment of decision to embark on an art-response experience, persons may become alert to resources of fine arts that could enlarge the teaching-learning opportunities in the group. These may take the form of photographs, designs, colorful magazine advertisments suggesting art forms or ideas, material from picture files and resource packets, magazine articles, selected nature objects, or flat or projected pictures that can be borrowed. A substantial amount of material can be utilized to provide for sufficient rotation from session to session, to offer a wide range of appeal, and to include potential correlation with biblical material that will be read (see Saturation Sally in Part 2).

You may wish to secure one or more shallow boxes of generous length and width to house your growing collection, for well-chosen material may have ongoing value for later use. After the experience gets under way and the group has an opportunity to become aware of what it is all about, they may be invited to bring in resources for display. Whatever has the potential to contribute to the growth of thought or the development of processes in the group may find a place. For more specific discussion of the uses of these resources, refer to the discussion in a later chapter (Saturation Sally in Part 2).

The personal-growth dimension is so vital to the art-response experience that its measure would be the only yardstick for evaluating any teaching-learning resulting from this method. Perhaps one reality which the Christian educator or minister is often tempted to wish he could change is the fact that there is no concrete tool for measuring the changes which occur in persons, that is, the growth that God brings about as confrontations with the gospel occur. We pray and work and plan, we study and innovate and program, we develop curriculum, we create settings, we provide materials, we reach out for persons to claim them for God, we yearn after them and agonize over their dilemmas, and yet when we look to see what has happened, we seldom can see or know about any dramatic or obvious changes.

God is so patient and we are so impatient! Part of our role

as servants through whom God can work is to accept the miracle that he is the doer and not we ourselves. We plant, we water, but "God [gives] the growth." And the measure of what he does is seldom known to us. But this does not mean that we do not set goals — very specific goals — and it does not mean that we should not continually and carefully evaluate, insofar as possible on the basis of whatever fragmentary evidence we can gather, to what extent we are achieving our purposes. Quite the contrary!

There are personal-growth dimensions for which we can work and hope as we move along in a group where opportunity is being given for art response to the Bible. *Only what is happening to people has real significance.* Although we cannot measure the extent of this happening, we need to focus our thinking upon some of the kinds of growing that persons may be doing, reminding ourselves that our primary purpose in using this teaching-learning method is *neither to impart knowledge* about the Bible *nor to produce striking art pieces,* but rather to provide opportunities for "dynamic interaction between the gospel and the concerns of the learner in the whole field of his relationships." [5]

Some educators have referred to this as the "crossing point." For any given person this is a point of insight, of "striking fire," of conviction, a moment at which ideas explode into new meanings which directly touch the life-need of that person. This is the moment at which a meaning dawns, and suddenly some facet of the gospel strikes upon an issue in that person's life and he appropriates that meaning for his becoming; he assimilates it for his value system, his decision making, his action, his philosophy, his attitudes.

The concept may be illustrated by two lines that intersect many times and at many intervals as they flow on and on. The first line represents the never-ending richness and depth and range of the gospel as it confronts a man time after time in many situations and places. The second line represents the life of the growing individual with its complexities of issues and immediate developmental tasks.

[5] *The Church's Educational Ministry:* A Curriculum Plan, The Work of Cooperative Curriculum Project (Bethany Press, 1965), p. 816, "Crossing Points."

the life
the gospel

Each point at which the individual becomes freshly aware of the meaning of the gospel for his life thus might be described as a "crossing point."

There are four areas of a person's character in which expansion or increase of personal-growth dimensions can be observed or noted, if we will look closely for these signs of maturing:

• *The Sense of God's Presence, Bringing About an Impact on Thinking, Feeling, and Behavior.* Opening the heart to God as we listen to the Bible takes us beyond the point of knowing "about" God in a secondhand fashion; we are not listening to opinions about or criticisms of the Bible, or absorbing material predigested by the leader and reorganized by him. Rather, we are responding directly to what is being said in the Bible and experiencing directly in God's presence what is significant for our own lives. Each person is free to respond in his own way to what is meaningful to himself. This should result in a firsthand rather than a secondhand acquaintance with God.

I OFFER MY PRAISE

The God of the Bible is a Lord of Joy, a Lord of Power and Action, the Lord of Love. As we open our thoughts to him, contemplate him, and are still — we KNOW THAT HE IS GOD, and at some point in our contemplation he "strikes fire" within us, and we must respond in praise which rises from our inmost being. This is a feeling-response, triggered by a feeling-impact, and a thought-response, triggered by a thought-impact. It is a mystical experience, a momentary joining of the self to the Infinite God, a losing of ourselves in him.

A high school senior, caught up in the glory of such an experience on a morning when we responded to Psalm 150 through the medium of paper cutting and pasting (*schnitzen*), stayed after the others had gone to say simply, "I really felt the Joy

of the Lord this morning!" We had all felt it; there was an atmosphere and spirit ascending into a climax of worship as we listened and worked. God was there and we knew it. He was there and we responded with hearts and minds as well as with fingers.

I OFFER MY WORK

As we respond with minds and feelings and fingers, we create a record of some facets of our total experience. Each individual, as he works with art materials in response to hearing the Bible, will pick out of a passage what is real for him, what he knows, not what a leader tells him he *should* know. Through *doing*, his horizons will expand. But there is far more going on within ourselves than will ever meet the eye. God is fully capable of bringing about ongoing changes in us as persons when we have experienced a confrontation with him. We can never be quite the same. If we accept what he can do for us and with us and in us, we move toward our potential for becoming, even though it may be only to an infinitesimal degree.

The work we offer in response may be but a symbol of the response we may bring him in our everyday living yet to come — in our thinking, in our feeling, and in our behavior.

33

I OFFER MY REACHING

Can we stir up a hungering and thirsting for God by exposing persons to contact with him in the pages of the Bible? Can we develop a listening-for-him, a sensitivity to his presence, a reaching for more of him? This should be an aim of a Christian teaching-learning experience — not to provide all the neatly packaged little answers, but to send off each person on a restless, driving quest for a more frequent and more continuous experience of communion with God.

A growing sense of familiarity with what the Bible has to say, the discovery that it speaks to me personally not exactly as it does to every other person, to me because I am me, and to me in different ways at different times because at that moment I am open to hearing what God has to say in the light of my immediate situation: these discoveries may lead me to want more of the experience of God.

Growing is a gradual thing, and as I grow, becoming aware that my attitudes, feelings, and understandings are changing, I become capable of more growing. I reach, and grow, *reach and grow*, REACH AND GROW.

• *The Sense of Self-Worth, of Self-Discovery, of Unrealized Potential.* One of the amazing aspects of the art-response experience is the element of self-discovery that can come to the participants. In the atmosphere of acceptance and appreciation, of valuing the individual as a person who is unique in his response, it is possible to see yourself afresh. So often the person with verbal skills carries off the day, receives the commendation of the "teacher" for coming forth with right answers or well-expressed perceptions, reads with expression for all to hear, and causes the less verbally oriented member of the group to pull self-consciously into his shell. Often this very person has something to say with his clay or his felt-tip marker when there is a democratic equalizing of opportunity for expression! And furthermore we discover that when he explains what he has done or talks about it, sometimes he has a very fine insight to share.

A number of these persons whose self-picture is of rather inept individuals, because so much of our recognition of persons is based on their language skills, approach the art-response experience with a "I'm not very good at this kind of thing" attitude. But in the warmth of encouragement which comes not

34

for skillful execution but for the idea behind it, and in the sense of achievement that comes from the freeing experience of finding acceptance and appreciation, these persons can discover something very basic about their own value.

Interestingly enough, though the verbally oriented person is frequently also free with art materials in response to hearing the Bible read, there are times in which the person who reads "like a wiz," and has always been the class star in discussion sessions, finds himself less able to translate his thoughts into art forms than the stumbling reader whose murderous pronunciation of words has always caused stifled giggles.

Such a child was Bobby, the fourth grader who was a very self-conscious participant in his first art-response session. When it was his turn to show and share the work he had done, he blurted out in explanation of his few, uncertainly executed forms, "I just didn't know what to put!" He readily regained his composure, however, when the teacher responded, "That's perfectly all right, Bobby. I noticed how very closely you were listening, and that is what is really important. Tell us what the greatest idea you heard this morning was, or what you liked best about the story." Here he was at home — with words. He should gain freedom in his art response in coming sessions, and thus grow in a sense of self-worth.

• *The Development of Skills in Communication.* There is an element of sensitivity training in the art-response approach, for one of the principles of the method is that we assume the value of each person and his capacity to contribute through being himself. We therefore seek to grow in appreciating other persons, perhaps in really seeing them for the first time, in responding with gentleness and the desire to understand what they are saying through their work. This creates a sense of "groupness," an unusual opportunity for group interaction, and the development of new relationships with other persons.

In response to the Sermon on the Mount, one teenager spent her entire time molding clay into a very lovely foot. As she shared with the group, she began, "Jesus walked up on the mountain. And the whole sermon is about how we should walk, and how we should follow him." Not one person in the group smiled nor intimated in any way that they noticed she had created a foot with only four toes! So tremendous was her idea,

35

so sincerely executed, and so basically beautiful, that the group responded with appreciation and communicated this to her in their attitude, without any words.

• *Satisfaction in Expressing Initiative, in Creativity, and in Contributing to Group Living.* Much of today's living tends to turn us into spectators rather than participants. This can be true of what is intended to be education. In addition to the opportunities for creative work with art materials, the art-response method offers persons many ways to exercise their initiative in following special interests. Developing such interests leads to personal growth and contributes to group living.

Students may follow their individual interests and become involved in music selection. They may find and bring in pictures or objects to add to the room atmosphere or for display during the Saturation Sally. Collecting or contributing "scrap material" for constructive use will be a source of great satisfaction to the ecology minded, and there is much room for using such material in the art-response experience. Students may work out uses for visual-aid equipment, assist in setting it up, and develop slides or tapes, implementing their own ideas and those of the group.

The dimensions of the Bible, Art, and Personal Growth have been sorted out for the sake of examination, but it is perfectly clear that they cannot be sorted out as they happen . . . for they are too intermingled, each too much a part of the others.

It is helpful, however, in planning and carrying through an experience in art response to the Bible to be aware of each dimension, and to view in the light of each what is happening in the group.

36

Part 2
PROJECTING A SESSION

An effective plan for a session of an art-approach experience may be developed by giving attention to five basic parts, each making a distinctive contribution to the whole. The session should provide an onward-flowing, inward-and-outward-growing, warmly glowing experience, with each of the five parts differently paced but each definitely related to the purposes of the session. You may want to develop your own terminology for each of these, but here for the sake of easy reference and to suggest the kind of thing which may be contained in each we shall assign these names to the parts:

1. Early Involvement
2. Saturation Sally
3. Reading and Response
4. Sharing and Analysis
5. Windup

These steps in sequence should be followed consistently for a most effective session, but the length of time used for each may vary considerably from one session to another. A good rule of thumb to keep in mind is this: Well over half the total time always should be allotted to Reading and Response, which is a major and fundamental section of activity.

How is the leader involved before the session begins? How can he offer the students invitations to involvement? How can he help them to begin to get involved?

THE LEADER'S INVOLVEMENT BEFORE THE SESSION

For many settings in the educational ministry of the church, a large number of leaders spend extensive time preparing for the group's teaching-learning experience. For those same settings, other leaders spend practically no time. All too familiar a note is struck by the picture of the teacher who arrives in the classroom after some of the students are already there, who then for the first time opens his teacher's text to the session marked for that day and begins to get involved in activities, often finding it necessary to uninvolve students with whatever they've dreamed up while they've been waiting. This "too little, too late" involvement sabotages *any* session, including the session in which the art-response approach is to be used. Any idea that this new approach to teaching-learning eliminates the need for preparation should be dispelled here and now, once and forever!

The leader must be involved in reading and rereading the Bible passage well in advance of the session to see what the Bible says to *him*, to reach for meanings. He may want to read it in several versions, to read it silently and aloud, to read commentaries, to look up places on a map, to find out how to pronounce names correctly and easily, to become familiar with Bible customs, lands, life, and times as related directly to the chapters or paragraphs to be included in the coming session. He may want to outline the material by paragraphs, to master its content thoroughly, to memorize one or more of its verses, to meditate on an idea that particularly intrigues or inspires him.

This does *not* mean he is preparing to share all of this with the group. It *does* mean he is getting excited about it, he is making it his own, he is discovering what is there, he is listening for God to speak to him, he is searching and praying and coming closer to realizing the presence of God in his own life, he is being confronted by meanings which have significance for him, he is coming to grips with concepts that are new to him.

It does *not* mean that he is consulting a predigested presentation of the possibilities for the session. It *does* mean that he is opening windows and exploring avenues of approach. He is thinking how the group may respond in art materials and in feelings and commitments.

This early involvement leads him to begin gathering pictures and objects to be used in the Saturation Sally; to think of ideas which may become a part of the prayer period, Opening the Heart to God; to choose recordings that will contribute to the mood of the session; to plan features and innovations which will intensify the experience.

A stenographer's notebook is ideal for laying out your session plans in advance. It may stand or lie open for easy reference in presenting clearly your ideas for the smooth movement of the experience, and may have in the corner (perhaps upper right) a list of everything needed in the line of materials for that specific session. Or you may find it helpful to underline with fine felt-tip marker in one color all the items you need to have ready for use, making an underline again at whatever point the items first occur in your plan. Or use whatever methods of planning and outlining may be most natural for you.

A leader's other early involvement is with the concerns he has for each of the students. Through studying a student's *Profile in Participation* (see section in Part 4: Tools for Planning), or whatever other tool may have been employed for knowing ahead of time the students who will be participating in the course; through careful observation of the response being given to the experiences offered; through alertness to the facts of individual interest, the signs of individual need, and the events in the lives of individual persons, the leader can focus procedures and content to have the highest significance for members of the group.

The leader brings together these two involvements — his early involvement with the biblical passage and his involvement with the individual students — in creating an atmosphere for HAPPENING.

CREATING AN ATMOSPHERE

In setting up the space for the session, the leader visualizes the flow from one activity to another. Materials and equipment are arranged in the space in such a way that there is imparted an air of expectation and of readiness. What is there and how it is there should issue an invitation to participate, to get involved. The room should always look at least a little different from the way it did when it was first seen in the preceding session, and often it may be markedly different. Variety gives freshness to the situation, and the surprise element stimulates creativity. God refuses to bring into being two flowers that are exactly alike, and dull, drab, unimaginative sameness could scarcely be an appropriate expression of love for him. Moving tables and chairs into new juxtaposition can be an act of worship. Placing a book where it will ask to be read can be a prayer. Putting a question on the board, hanging a poster, or a display of musical instruments on a pegboard — these can be loving services done in praise to God.

The atmosphere of the setting is created by the total effect of a myriad of small things that say, "Something exciting and wonderful can happen here — in fact, is about to happen!" "There is so much to discover, to feel, to do, to know!" "God cares. . . ." "The church cares." One teenager expressed his wonder to the teacher of an art-response course thus, "It's wonderful that somebody will go to all this trouble for us."

It's in things as small as sharpened pencils and clean sponges, and as big as a wall covered with striped ticking to which have been pinned the colorful collages made the week before in response to the Shepherd Psalm — a really breathtaking confrontation!

OPENING THE HEART TO GOD

The first fruitful act of togetherness in every session can be moments of prayer spoken for all to share. Here are a few of the many ways this can be done:

Each person may write a sentence prayer and then read it in turn.

Read a prayer in unison from the board or from prepared sheets.

Have one person read a prayer that has been prepared ahead of time.

Have one person read a psalm, as 139, or a prayer from the Bible. (The person reading should have practiced ahead of time so that the words will flow meaningfully.)

Provide a sheet of paper on which a prayer has been lettered sentence by sentence with spaces between cut almost completely across. As the group is seated in a circle or around a table, one person can walk around, quickly tearing off a section for each seated person. Since these are passed out in sequence, the fragmented prayer becomes whole again as all participate in reading in the same order around the table. (See the following page.)

40

Dear God, Our Father:
A lot of things have happened in our lives
since last we met here together.

We thank you for all the moments when
you have been caring for us and helping
us and we have realized this.

We ask you to forgive us for all the moments
you've been ready to help us but we have
ignored or forgotten you.

And forgive us for all the hours you
have been caring for us but we have
been living with only thoughts of ourselves, and we've made bad decisions.

We're here now to enjoy being together,
to enjoy what we can do, to think new
thoughts, and most of all, to discover
you.

Put your thoughts into our minds.

Put your feelings into our hearts.

Thank you for your patience with us
and for your love which has given
us Christ to show us your way
and how to live.

Help us to think, and to commit
our minds, hearts, souls, and strength
to you.

                    Amen.

An example of an opening prayer used with teenagers.

41

God, you are here with us now, and we know it!

Give us quietness inside ourselves so we can listen for you. . . .

Everything you have done to make this a beautiful spring day is GOOD—the sun, the tulips in the square, spring waking the world to green and gold, people who CARE, the fellowship of all who love you, truth, your Book waiting to be read so you can speak to us through its meanings.

But so much of what man has done is NOT GOOD . . .

men dying in the jungles,

hungry children,

parents fighting with one another,

people grabbing for THINGS,

people having hangovers from last night.

Help us to be YOURS, TRULY YOURS, to live and think and grow in your way.

Amen

SOME OTHER PRAYERS

Here we are together again, Lord, waiting to hear what you will say to us to respond with things to . . .

Clear our minds of clutter so we can think the thoughts you'd give us. Help us to find some answers we are looking for, and to begin to ask some new questions. We praise you for your love. Put that love to work in our lives to change us and to stir us to love other persons.

amen

These are but suggestions. You will think of many other ways to provide variety. It is important to set the tone for the session by experiencing prayer that is spontaneous, sincere, and planned, so that there can be a mood of reverence, of quiet seeking, and of frank and open honesty.

This somewhat peculiar designation was born out of searching for terminology that would describe two aspects of the purpose of this part. "Saturation" carries the idea of soaking up, of absorbing all that the mind and feelings can hold, to become completely penetrated by what is offered; "Sally" describes an excursion or adventure away from the usual track, a sortie, a bursting forth, a flight of fancy, a lively leaping of the mind and spirit.

A Nonverbal Period

This block of time provides for a period of personal meditation and communion with God. It is a time for stirring up thoughts and feelings, for unfolding the mind to fresh ideas. Although there is a very real sense of fellowship with other members of the group, the experience is completely nonverbal. It is simply amazing how responsive persons are to this opportunity for freedom from words. In our culture, full to overflowing, crammed to overcapacity with the continuous bombardment of words upon our minds, even the most talkative of teenagers and children have no problem in sublimating or relieving their urge to talk and substituting silence. The pressure to talk is off; the acceptability of silence is on. Through this Saturation Sally period and on through the Reading and Response period, the energy that would be expended normally either in talking, in waiting with frustration for a turn to talk, or in worrying because you may appear stupid for not talking or may say the wrong thing, is channeled and stored in nonverbal participation. It is released in the art-response opportunity immediately to follow. It is like storing water in a dam ready to spill out when the sluice is opened. It builds to an on-tiptoe, ready-to-go feeling that enriches the outflowing of thought and emotion through art materials as the Bible is read.

SEEING[1]

A primary stimulus to thinking and feeling comes through seeing. What we see can stir in us tremendous tides of emotion and bring to our minds an amazing range of thought. How we respond in thought and feeling to what we see is determined by our potential for response and also by all the experiences which have been ours up to the precise moment of seeing. This is therefore a highly individualized response, and the seeing that is done in the Saturation Sally is free from the bondage of being told by a teacher *what we should see* in whatever we are looking at, or from the distraction of having to listen to what other people say they are seeing. We can just *look*, and *think*, and *feel*.

Materials arranged to invite the eye will be primarily two dimensional — flat pictures and maps — with some use of objects, books, projected materials, mobiles. Criteria for selecting materials to be offered are suggested by these questions:

- Is it appealing in line, color, depth, texture?
- Will it stimulate thoughts about the meaning and purpose of
    Existence?
    God's self-disclosure?
    Redemption?
    Discipleship?
    Christian Community? [2]
- Can it enrich our background for meaningful listening to the biblical text to be used in this session? [3]
- Does it suggest art techniques which may enrich the individual's response with art materials?

Teaching packets from past curriculum studies will be a good source, but material displayed should not be limited to choices

[1] See page 30 for discussion of types of art, and suggestions for collecting and storing these.

[2] Study pages viii and ix and paragraphs 43 through 245 of *The Church's Educational Ministry* (St. Louis: Bethany Press, 1965) for a clearer understanding of these questions. Select for study any sections in the balance of the book (sections 259-784) that apply to the age group participating in this course.

[3] See the Biblical Dimension in Part 1 for examples of biblical enrichment materials.

from these. Current religious publications and secular magazines are also rich sources. Pages should be trimmed to show only what is intended for impact, and they should be mounted or pasted back-to-back so that no triviality impinges, even if the pieces are turned over.

Except for an occasional session in which all materials are related to a central theme, as is true of the examples on page 22 what is offered should have a real cross section of appeal in style and subject. Books should have a marker placed at the section which proposes a focus, or should lie open. One or more Bibles are usually included. Much of what is displayed will be from the contemporary scene, and frequently a line of large print which stimulates thought is already printed on the sheet. Two examples of this kind of choice:

PICTURED, a woman in blue face mask and curlers, and the line, "You think it all happens on the outside?"

PICTURED, four cars of fresh vintage, and the words, "Man shall not live by four-door sedans alone."

As well as art of the masters or traditional art forms, there should be displayed art that is psychedelic, abstract, or contemporary, but each should be chosen with an eye to value rather than at random. Colorful clippings from current denominational publications have a place if you remember that pictorial rather than lettered material is the thrust.

Variety of shape is another important fact to keep in mind. A substantial proportion of the material will need to be cut and/or mounted on shapes other than the traditional parallel-sided rectangle. Nor need we be limited to geometric shapes: we can employ free-flowing lines which result in an assortment of abstracts and curves.

It is appropriate to select, prepare, and scatter-arrange materials for the Saturation Sally in a spirit of sensitivity, alertness, and prayer for God's guidance.

HEARING

A record player in good working order with a pleasing quality of tone reproduction is an essential piece of equipment for the Saturation Sally. Suggestions for a choice of music are to be found on page 29, "Music Listening," and page 81, "Suggested Appropriate Music Recordings."

Used as an alternate to or in addition to the record player may be a tape recorder. There is some merit in using the tape recorder if you have time to tape selected music in preparation for the session, and if you know your machine well enough to handle it smoothly and to control the volume.

Plan for between five and ten minutes playing time, including transition silence, since this will be about the total time available in a session of an hour.

FREEDOM TO MOVE, TO TOUCH, TO HANDLE

In arranging the room, allow sufficient space for moving around, for walking about the room to study display areas (which can be vertical or horizontal), for sitting down to study one particular item, for walking around a table for a better view of something that catches the eye, for standing in one place without obstructing another person's freedom to move or to look. Picking up a picture or object, handling it, touching it, moving it — all these are included in sharpening awareness and in responding with thought and emotion.

RECORDING THOUGHTS

An opportunity should be provided for recording a thought that any member of the group might want to remember or share, though this recording should be purely voluntary and individual. One or more shallow baskets of plain paper slips, about 2"x4" or 3"x5", should be placed near the viewing areas with pencils conveniently at hand. Anyone who wishes to do so may then use a pencil and paper to write down any idea that floods his mind and demands spilling over into expression.

Slips on which participants write may be kept by them or may be placed in another container to be used in whatever ways seem appropriate. Sometimes these have value for reading in closing moments or in opening moments of the next session. Some recorded thoughts may offer ideas to be incorporated into the course. Some might become copy for a parish paper or church bulletin, or might be duplicated on sheets or put into a booklet for a record of experiences during the course. Some groups like to have folders in which various materials from the

46

course may be placed, and others might like to put them on a tackboard as they are written. Anything that is written and made available by the person who wrote it should find a use whether it is shared anonymously or with identification. Using this kind of contribution recognizes the uniqueness of each person and his capacity for enriching the living of all.

These suggestions for the Saturation Sally should be carried out consistently in every session, at least throughout a course which the teacher has not had experience in the art-response techniques. Later, with growing understanding and practice, innovations will be devised which keep the purposes of the course clearly in mind. The block of time, kept as a period of nonverbal participation with enrichment opportunities to saturate the mind, is essential to the success of the session. Experimentation in the general use of the art-response method without including this part of the session has shown that the Saturation Sally contributes substantially to the freedom and productivity of the experience.

A few generations ago, "priming the pump" was a familiar figure of speech. Though the figure might have changed, the principle is still the same: Sometimes to get a free-flowing stream most easily, pour a little in! Saturation Sally pours a little in. . . .

We now come to the heart of the session, exposure to the ideas and messages of the Bible. These are offered without added comment or interpretation, but with the accompanying opportunity to respond, not in words but with art materials that are ready, waiting, inviting a response.

The preparation of mind which has preceded has laid a framework, and the atmosphere of love, acceptance, and concern has set the tone of freedom to respond in ways which are spontaneous and relevant to the individual. The readiness of materials and the leader's anticipation of the individual's needs will contribute to the individual's freedom of response and eliminate the need for interruptions to provide more space, more materials, more comfortable situations for persons as they work.

PRACTICAL SUGGESTIONS FOR MECHANICS

To anticipate the ways in which space and materials will be

used and to provide for these ways is to contribute an essential element to the success of the experience — success meaning the achievement of goals rather than the perfection of the finished art pieces.

Materials to be used must be provided in an adequate amount, and an additional supply must be conveniently near for persons freely but quietly to move to get whatever they feel they need in order to react to what they are hearing. Before the reading begins, there should be an understanding that if Jack needs blue paper or Leigh wants another piece of chalk it is all right to go and get the items they want, providing the group is not interrupted; movement should be achieved with a view to what other persons are doing, with respect and consideration for their flow of thought and freedom in expressing it.

It is helpful to have materials within easy reach and to have a basic supply obviously at hand on a nearby table or on shelves invitingly open.

Have everything ready. If your space is really adequate, the group can move from the Saturation Sally to the tables where art materials are arranged for work, and there will be no dispelling of the mood which has been created. But if space is limited, each person can clear the place where he chooses to work and put out his own work materials. This can be done quite easily providing the leader has boxes ready at the side to receive the visual materials which have just been used for the Saturation Sally and has art materials arranged in an orderly fashion, but sufficiently spread out, so that people can get what they need with little waiting. If you lack table space, a triple-deck, rolling cart is very helpful: an inexpensive one will serve the purpose.

Have the Disciplines (see page 10) conspicuously displayed. Vary their location. Use eye-catching forms and color for presenting them. You may want to make a new set after a few weeks, perhaps altering wording to include some new idea forthcoming from the group. Occasionally these may be read in unison, silently, or by one person as this part of the session begins.

The reader may be more effective if he reads from different locations in the room during a session for which more than one chapter is included; or if a passage is reread several times in different ways. There seems to be value in the variety offered by changes from session to session so that sometimes the reader sits at the back of the room, sometimes stands at the side, sometimes has a seat at the table with the group as the reading begins.

If there is a second adult on the teaching team, another element of variety may come in the ways in which the reading is shared. Or more helpful might be having the second person serve as an aide, ready to assist anyone who needs a fresh sheet of paper, a wet sponge for fingers, a refill of paste or a filled paper moved out of the way.

Be sure to leave enough time for the sharing period and the closing, even though the group may be having a productive and exciting time. The minutes allotted for these parts of the session may be sometimes shorter, sometimes longer, but if they are eliminated entirely the session misses a very important rounding out of experience.

THE READING OF THE BIBLE

Your ideas of making the Bible reading effective will grow as you work with this method of teaching-learning. The discussion of the Biblical Dimension (see pages 15-23) includes many helpful principles and suggestions you may want to keep in mind. This is a pivot around which the whole method moves.

SOME EXPERIENCES DESCRIBED [4]

Let us here describe in words and pictures what this part of the session may be like, with a sharp awareness, however, that each session is an event or a series of events which can never be duplicated — nor would we want them to be.

Example One

Passage to Be Read: Psalm 100
Art Method to Be Used: *Schnitzen* (see page 26)
Preparation of Room:
• On one wall a bedspread-size expanse of blue and white ticking has been hung, and to it are pinned with straight pins the pieces of work done the week before, each piece expressing a student's response to Psalm 23 (the *schnitzen* method was used).
• On another wall is a classroom-sized chalkboard (9 feet long)

[4] For other experiences see sections 24 and 38 of Part 3: Showcase of Ideas.

49

to which have been taped in an abstract form three rectangles of large construction paper each 24″ x 36″, one yellow-green, one rose, and one pale blue. These overlap at angles to produce one form.

• On the board tray is a piece of chalk; near at hand a Bible is open to Psalm 100.

• A table large enough to seat the entire group of students is arranged for work. A pair of scissors is at each place, and between each two places there is a plastic container of paste with two paste sticks. In the center of the table are shallow boxes of assorted colored papers, each cut to a working square about 5″; here also are half a dozen reference Bibles. Within reach of each student, damp sponges have been placed on waxed paper.

• On the supply table are additional scissors, scrap paper, another box of paper squares, more paste sticks and paste, extra chalk, crayons, felt-tip markers, pencils, three rulers, the record player and records.

Procedure:

Each student selects a square of paper; his scissors are poised to start. The reader begins with verse 1, reading slowly and expressively in a strong, clear voice. After a pause of perhaps five seconds, he rereads the same verse at a lower pitch, more gently, and with a varied expression.

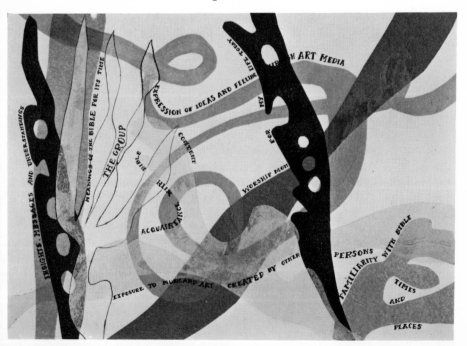

The reader remains silent for about a minute to permit time for the student to complete his cutout, lay it on the table, and pick up a second square for cutting in readiness for the reading of the next verse.

The reader reads verse 2 aloud as he did verse 1 — once in a strong, clear voice, then after a pause, he rereads more gently and with expression different from that of the first reading. While this is being read, the students respond by cutting forms from the second papers chosen.

Each student places this cutout on top of the first one.

The reading continues verse by verse or sentence by sentence, with students continually responding as they use square after square of paper.

When the psalm has been read thus, each student picks up his pile of cut forms, turns it over and studies each of his responses as the teacher slowly reads the psalm again.

There follows now a period of silence or of selected musical background while students, in whatever order and timing each one wishes, include these activities:

Cutting additional forms, perhaps with reference to an open Bible for rereading the psalm.

Applying paste to what he has cut and placing his cutouts on the prepared area of paper sheets.

Taking a turn to write or print a part of the psalm on the board: one student begins this, and as he lays down the chalk another student picks it up and goes on till the whole psalm is on the board.

Colored chalk may be used to embellish the open spaces on the board if anyone wishes to do this.

Example Two

Passage to Be Read: Nehemiah 4, 5, and 6.
Art Method to Be Used: Droodles (See page 25, felt-tip marker recordings.)
Preparation of Room:
• If the table surface that students are to use needs protection from bleed-through, cover the tables with newspaper from the

51

Sunday classified sections which give a rather plain, overall gray effect as a working surface.

• Between each two students place a paste cup and two sticks for adding on sections of paper as these are needed.

• Provide about three felt-tip markers for each two students. These may be placed in a small, shallow box between each pair of students.

• Cut strips of newsprint (plain) 6″ wide. The yield from each 18″ x 24″ sheet — the standard size — will be three strips, each 6″ x 24″. Plan an adequate supply; some students require three to

five of these in a session. Place a pile in the middle of each table within easy reach of every student.

• Walls may display groupings of abstract art, illustrations of the story of Nehemiah from your picture file, students' work from the preceding session.

• On the supply table are scissors, extra strips, extra paste, pencils, rulers, and any other supplies you have discovered to be basically useful.

Procedure:

Each student places his paper vertically before him on the table so that he is ready to work at the top end, the lower end extending off the table. As he works he will roll the paper that is finished, unless he has plenty of work space.

He letters at the top of his paper "Nehemiah 4," picks up the felt-tip marker of his choice, and is ready to start.

The reader begins reading aloud from the Bible (or a previously-made tape may be used for variety should you wish a different voice from the teacher's or the regular reader's.) A deliberate pace is important to provide students with the time needed for response. However, the reading need not drag, and can be quite brisk at times. Variety of expression, dramatic emphasis, variation in pitch and speed are important. Longer pauses may come between paragraphs. With the beginning of a new chapter, students letter "Nehemiah 5." If a chapter is long, the group members may indicate milestones whenever the reader cues them in by mentioning the verse he is about to read, but this should be done sparingly so that the flow of the story is not broken.

As students use nearly all of a strip, they should begin on a fresh one, leaving an inch or so overlap for pasting later.

When the reading is finished, each student pastes his strips end to end, forming one long strip, and rolls it with the beginning end out so that he is ready for the sharing time.

EXAMPLE THREE

Passages to Be Read: A key verse from each chapter of the book of the Acts of the Apostles; this book was completed in the previous session after several weeks of pursuing its text through the art-response method and this is a summary.

Method to Be Used: Crayon resist (See #12, Part 3: Showcase of Ideas.)

Preparation of Room:

• Provide for each student a set of crayons which includes basic colors and some tints and hues different from the usual eight sticks in the simple crayon box. These can be shared between two students if funds are limited. They should be in an open, shallow box.

• Provide also white and assorted colors of paper 12"x18", two sheets to a student. These may be arranged on the supply table where each student can make his own choice, folding each of the two pieces he selects in half once to create four 9"x12" surfaces for his work.

• A rack of tempera paints (or a plastic container or box of paint glasses) of assorted colors which are mixed to the correct consistency should be ready on the supply table, along with a stack of newspapers and enough ½" or ¾" brushes so that each member of the class may use one.

Special Preparation by the Teacher:

• Be ready to read in succession a key verse from each chapter selected carefully in advance either by you or by the suggestions of the students.

Procedure:

Give each student time to divide his four working surfaces each into seven areas or to plan how he will do this as he works. Chapters 1-7 will go on one surface, chapters 8-14 on the second, chapters 15-21 on the third, and chapters 22-28 on the fourth. Explain that these will be used as cover sheets for the notes and responses we have developed in this course.

Give the reference for the verse from chapter 1 as "Acts 1:8" and read the verse deliberately once. Pause and repeat the verse once. As you do so, students will use crayons to respond with some form which represents an idea this verse suggests to them.

Move along in order, using a verse from each chapter in the same manner. (This procedure is, of course, serving as a review of the book.)

54

When the Reading and Response is completed, each student may open his folded sheets and apply tempera of his choice in a wash over the surfaces, leaving them flat to dry completely.

Later these can be refolded to create two covers, the front cover beginning with chapter 1, and continuing the summary in sequence on the front inside cover, the back inside cover, and the back.

Showing what our responses have been adds many values to the experience of the group in this teaching-learning method. Each person has responded differently. Meanings and insights which persons reveal as they share their thinking, their ideas, and their feelings with the rest of the group enrich all.

INDIVIDUAL INSIGHTS

We have here an opportunity to appreciate the differences between us, and the comments of persons will bring us new thoughts which we shall not forget. One eighth grader began responding to the story of the good Samaritan by drawing first a fire, then a flower. The meaning of these forms was explained to the listening group thus: "First I drew a fire because the lawyer was testing him like a fire. And when Jesus answered, his answer was beautiful like a flower."

This eighth grader's response has enriched forever the understanding of the incident for any listener who really absorbed the ideas shared on this occasion.

RECALL

The Sharing and Analysis also serve as a review or a recall of what has been read. One boy prefaced his sharing of an idea with the comment, "I'm not very good at this sort of thing." The reading had been Matthew 5, 6, and 7, the Sermon on the Mount, and the response had been with salt-flour clay. He had shaped the letters F O O D, and decorated them with bits of eggshell. This seemed like a surprising response, but as we pursued his thinking many ideas came out. We recalled many references to food in the chapters: hungering and thirsting for righteousness, and being satisfied . . . salt . . . "Give us this day our daily bread" . . . fasting . . . "Do not be anxious . . . what you shall eat" . . . "Is not life more than food?" . . . "Your heavenly

Father feeds them." . . . "Do not be anxious saying, 'What shall we eat?'" . . . "But seek first his kingdom" . . . a loaf, not a stone . . . a fish, not a serpent . . . grapes and thistles . . . good fruit and evil fruit . . . and all of Jesus' words, food for the spirit, and food for thought . . . !

BEAUTY

In addition to our enjoyment of form and color, of texture, of depth, of line, of the creative potential each person revealed in his expression of response, we have experienced deepening of meanings, fresh insights, sharper memory. The dimensions of personal growth are so accurately revealed in conjunction with the biblical dimension and the art dimension that each sharing and analysis period simultaneously becomes a time of special value to every participant.

DISCUSSION

Sometimes comments will come in response to the sharing of one person and a discussion of the passage will develop, or the sharing will lead to delineating something especially significant to all. It is impossible to predict how God may speak, but it is exciting — truly exciting!

Sometimes questions will be raised which require a return to the text, or a look ahead to see what is coming in the next session. Sometimes we may bring to light something we want to look up before or at the beginning of the next session.

And often there is opportunity to highlight or accent some major purpose of the passage, some basic idea, some flow of thought. The leader will discover that his saturation with the passage, his meditation on it, his background reading, his personal involvement with its message is called into use on some of these occasions in a sentence here, a question there, a word of appreciation for the discovery a student has made.

The interchange of ideas and responses contributes to a sense of "groupness," and leads naturally into the closing moments of the session.

LABELING AND DISPLAYING

Before leaving the section Sharing and Analysis, we might call attention to the fact that looking at what we have done and talking about it can lead to ideas of ways we want to display it or store it. Someone may come up with an idea for arranging what has been done in order to display it to the best advantage. Someone else may have an idea about a technique or procedure which could be followed in the coming session. An exhibit of the work may develop for the conclusion of the course. Ways of labeling, composing of a legend, creative writing, notes for the church paper or bulletin, or notices for the bulletin board may grow out of the Sharing and Analysis.

Members of the entire fellowship of the church can have a share in the experiences of the group as they are made aware of what is going on through:

occasional reporting in church papers or parish publications,

appeals for materials that can be contributed,

receiving opportunity to see work that has been produced.

What is an effective way to conclude the session? What experiences will summarize the session or offer a bridge to the next? Are there ways of emphasizing the impressions of the experience? What is the best way to handle the process of getting the space back into order? What about evaluation?

MOMENTS FOR MEDITATION

A brief period for personal reflection on the meanings which the session has brought into focus has proven to be the most effective experience for concluding the session.

In a number of instances where the art-response experience has been used, each group has provided its own guidance for what will best serve such purposes. In some a consistent pattern was preferred; in others, procedures varied from week to week. It is appropriate to include some form of prayer, whatever else may be included. Here are a few ways that have worked effectively:

• *The Endless Prayer Chain.* Joining hands in an unbroken circle around the work table (in the center of which a lighted candle has been placed), the group stands with heads bowed while the leader, or a person designated to do so, voices a prayer for all.

• *A Summary Statement and Silent Prayer.* The statement

57

should be written or chosen ahead of time; sometimes a poem or a hymn (using only the words) may be found which has special relationship to the major ideas of the Bible passage around which the session was planned. On occasion the statement might be written during the Sharing and Analysis. Several moments of silent prayer may be concluded with an audible "Amen."

• *Spontaneous Prayer.* Some groups are responsive to the opportunity to express thoughts aloud to God; in other groups, all might be given a few moments to write a sentence or two, and then any who wish could read aloud the prayers that have been written.

• *Silent Reflection Followed by Unison Prayer.*

• *A Choral Reading or a Prayer Read Responsively.*

In most cases three to five minutes is adequate for this quiet time. It should offer a high moment of awareness of the presence of God, cannot be permitted to become routine, and will be varied in style from the prayer experience at the beginning of the session.

At times the meditation could be a few moments in sharing "What the session meant to me," or "Things I wondered about today," or "Something I thought about since I came in," or "A question that has been raised in my mind." A sense of being close to one another and close to God is the hopeful mood.

LOOKING AT THE NEXT SESSION

Before the group breaks up, there may be mention of some experience coming in the next session: This could involve content, personalities, procedures, or needed materials. Any special responsibilities to be assumed or interim involvement to be appropriated should be called to the attention of persons who might wish to be a part of such participation.

If questions have been raised, suggestions made, or interests expressed, be sure to make a note of these so there can be provision for following through on them.

CLEANUP

No one procedure can be suggested which will be best for every group, but obviously this part of the experience calls for good planning on the part of the group.

58

Some groups may want to proceed on an "everyone-do-your-own" basis. Others may want to rotate responsibilities. Still others may want to plan for persons who participate in the course to assume the kinds of roles which appeal most to each. Whatever plan is decided upon will need to be made clear to the whole group so that clean-up procedures move with a minimum of directions. In some cases this can be accompanied by a "coffee-time," "coke-time," or "music-time" fellowship period for those who want to be leisurely about leaving; again this will be determined by the needs and interests of the group.

If roles are assumed, these might include some of the following:

Media Chairman/Media Committee, responsible for storage of art material

Music Chairman/Music Committee, care of record player and records

Librarian, storage of books and Bibles

Prop Man, arrangement of furniture

Log Keeper, records of attendance, minutes of activities, and group decisions. The Log Keeper also will care for written proceedings of the group, contacting an ill member, writing thanks to a visiting resource person, or similar duties.

The leader who assumes the responsibility for an art-response course, or who uses this method of teaching, may as well face from the outset the fact that there is real honest-to-goodness work involved in the windup of the session as well as in the preparation for it. But this windup time, when utilized cooperatively by the members of the group, can result not only in space ready for its next use, materials satisfactory for coming use, and art work respected and put away carefully, but in knowing better the persons who share in the work. The personal dimension is always a major one, and the casual exchange of ideas and comments can result in closer relationships between "learners" and "teachers" — for all participants have both roles!

Part 3
SHOWCASE OF IDEAS

To spur your thinking and to prime your creativity, we suggest in this section an array of possible approaches and activities for a course which may be structured in the art-response teaching-learning experience, or for use in a more traditional course in the church's educational program.

This will suggest ways for adapting techniques to the purpose of providing confrontations with the meanings and the message of the Bible. Here you will make a small beginning toward discovering the vast array of experiences possible for persons who embark on this adventure in freeing others to respond with mind, hand, and feeling to what the Bible says to them.

As your mind begins to strike sparks, be sure to have a pencil in hand and add your own notes to this section or make spontaneous jottings in a notebook.

1. Provide sheeting or unbleached muslin on which responses may be recorded with crayons. After work is completed, press these with a warm iron, crayoned surface facedown against plain paper. Fringed or bordered, these become wall hangings. Some examples of passages for this kind of experience are: Job 38; Psalm 19; Luke 8, the parable of the sower, or divide the chapter into three or four sections and use each parable; Isaiah 35; John 15.

2. Use realia, that is, real objects, for the Saturation Sally, and feature materials that have a relationship to the passage on which the session is focused. For instance, for Psalm 104 display bird's nest, stones, feathers, grass, bowl of water, branches, bird in a cage, fruit, leaves, bottle of oil, wineglass of grapejuice, twig or bough of fir or cedar, slice of bread, small metal box of dust, flat of plants or potted plants, basket of vegetables. Use background music of nature sounds: water, wind, birds.

60

For use with 2 Chronicles 1–7, purple, crimson and blue fabrics; cedar wood and boughs; scent boxes of spices; gourds, palms, chains; bar of iron; carved gold, silver, and bronze; pomegranate; diagram of early Hebrew measuring system; lily; jewels; compass; wash basin; handleless cup; pitcher with wick to represent lamp; linen; small iron pot, shovel, fork; trumpet, cymbals; candle snuffer; tongs; wool; bread. Incense could be burning, and background music would be early stringed instruments, harp, or trumpet.

3. Make a character collage. Read passages from the Bible that relate events in the life of some person. Provide boxes of scrap material of assorted textures from which each student can select, shape, and arrange textures and forms which seem to him to suggest the character of that person. (This will not be representational in the sense of posing a physical likeness of the character but rather will be representative of his qualities of life and personality, what makes him essentially himself). After members of the group have shared their finished work and ideas, it might be valuable to make a list of characteristics, giving examples of what in the text delineated each.

Good characters for this sort of thing might be Peter, John, Elijah, Jacob, Ruth, Solomon, or Mary.

4. Invite resource persons to share in the course. Meeting persons is enriching, and each has something distinctive to contribute to the living and thinking of the group. The guest will also be enriched by sharing with the group. Some areas for enrichment may be explored by inviting:

Guest Readers — to provide variety of voice timbre and expression as we listen to the reading of the Bible.

Instrumentalists — to stimulate our thinking and feeling for a period of meditation and discovery.

Travelers — to share observations, pictures, and knowledge of Bible lands on a focused and relevant matter.

A fellow Christian — to guide in the opening or closing moments of the session as we pray, search within, and lift our thoughts to God and to the world outside ourselves.

An artist — to demonstrate a technique and to show work

61

produced through employing this technique.

And others?

5. Free yourself from being limited to the rectangle as a shape on which responses may be recorded. Other forms can offer variety and stimulate fresh creativity. Introduce the use of non-rectangles. You could:

> Provide each student with a series of circles for recording responses to the creation story, using one for each "day";
>
> Provide a cross of generous proportions for each person to record his responses to the account of Passion Week — Mark 11–16 or Luke 19–24;
>
> Provide large "tables of stone," shaped boards on which to record responses to the Ten Commandments;
>
> Use hexagons or octagons for a passage from an epistle;
>
> Encourage students to cut their own free-flowing forms by shaping paper with scissors.

6. Offer an exhibit of the work of the course at its completion. Let students arrange their work; letter legends, signs, and markers to explain what was done; act as "guides" to answer questions; serve coffee or punch; select and play background music during the exhibit; write notices for publicity, make posters announcing the display. (A piece done in the course may be used as a poster when it is mounted and has added lettering to accompany it.)

7. Have a session of "Verse Happenings," letting each student in turn read a verse he has specially selected in advance. Responses to this experience might be recorded in many ways. One appropriate idea is to provide a series of squares for each student. On each he will pencil his response to a single verse, (also writing the reference somewhere on the sheet); later he can staple his "set" into a booklet or sew them, adding a cover sheet. Paint or felt-tip marker are also effective media in place of a pencil: a striking result is achieved through mounting finished work on the sides of boxes to be stacked, or taping it to bottles or round cartons, such as potato chip or ice cream containers.

8. Use scrap materials to make mosaics. Interesting expression of responses will result from having a supply of basic chips cut before the reading begins. Then provide each student with scissors and material to cut special shapes as the reading proceeds; he can combine these as he wishes, but can work more quickly by using the ready-cut shapes as fill-ins. Consider fabric as well as paper and eggshells or stones. Backgrounds can be of board, plywood scraps, or salt-flour clay plaques, still wet.

9. Do not overlook the possibilities of finger painting, either as a medium for use early in the experience to encourage freedom of participation or for use later on, especially for passages which seem to project a dominant mood — joy, confession and cleansing, sorrow, turmoil, etc. If the passage is not of great length, read it while the group listens with closed eyes. Then let each select his color(s) and work during a second reading.

10. Use newspaper pages of classified ads for work with felt-tip marker droodles or paint. This background is especially effective for readings from books of history, law, or the prophets.

11. Do you have a photographer in the group? Or can you involve one as an auditor, perhaps combining his participation with operating the record player? If not, can you have on hand a simple flash camera for use at the moments when you would like a photographic recording of an experience-event? One group, having done collages of Psalm 150 on a spring morning, carried the work out to the grass, and, placing an open Bible on a rock landscaped with tulips in a setting of budding branches, made a color slide. Casual rather than posed shots are usually best, and pictures which feature one center of interest rather than trying to get everything in are more successful, although the example above is obviously one of the other type!

12. Use crayon-resist technique. This method is appropriate for responding to any passage. Students will apply crayon brightly and heavily to the selected paper surface during the reading. When it is complete, each person will choose whatever tempera color he prefers and apply a thin coat of this over the total picture. (See page 54 for an example.)

13. For a Saturation Sally create a startling effect by arranging among pictures of ancient objects "scrabbles" of paper in bright colors. Cut these in shapes and curls, wadding and folding to add interest and texture.

14. As you make ready to read materials aloud, part of your preparation could be to outline or diagram the passage(s) in a notebook or on plain paper. Mark your Bible in any way that will help you to remember observations, insights, fresh ideas that strike you.

15. Invite the group to bring in materials which will contribute to the experience of the course, such as:

art materials   examples of contemporary or ancient art
scrap materials   recordings on records or tapes

16. Read from different versions or translations of the Bible to add vividness and understanding. Borrow a wide selection of these as well as Bibles of different sizes and types, and provide this display for browsing and study for at least one Saturation Sally during the course.

17. When separate papers or sections of paper have been planned for different passages being read successively in a single session, you can indicate the time to move to the next section by using a prearranged signal that will not interrupt the mood. A pleasing musical tone will be best for this. In some cases the passages themselves will seem to suggest what will be the most appropriate choice. This is not to become a gimmick, so you may want to stick to one choice for this sort of thing throughout the course. Possibilities are use of bells, a triangle, a note on a xylophone or tone blocks, striking a tom-tom, or even tapping a glass that has a pleasant tone.

This plan is helpful also when the reader wishes to indicate he is moving to a new paragraph, a new chapter, or a new verse, providing this information will be useful to the listeners in structuring their responses.

MOBILES

18. Individual or cooperative mobiles offer dramatic possibilities for a response which can be visible in ongoing form. Provide the material from which forms for the mobiles can be cut, and give time during the Reading and Response for spontaneous cutting out of freehand forms. The wire, sticks, thread, or other material for assembling mobiles can be provided for taking home to finish, then brought back for sharing. Or time may be allowed at the beginning of the session the following week for arranging and balancing the mobiles. This last part of the process is time-

consuming; while it is in progress, the passage being translated into art-language may be reread.

19. Encourage students to own and read their own Bibles. Each person will do well to purchase a copy of *Good News for Modern Man,* Today's English Version of the New Testament, which in paperback edition costs only pennies per copy. You might have copies available on hand to sell.

20. Plan to use the crayon-etching technique. As students arrive, they may go to work covering the entire surface of the paper to be used for this session's response with many colors of crayons, applying these brightly, solidly. After patting this colored surface with chalk dust from a board eraser, black crayon is applied over the entire colored area and polished with a rag until it is glossy.

Provide pointed tools, such as crochet hooks, nails, corsage pins, tapestry needles. Put these prepared materials aside until after the Saturation Sally.

As the reading begins, responses of each student are recorded by him on his own paper by scratching the prepared surface with the sharp tools. The more etching done, the more interesting and complete the work will be, and the more texture it will assume.

21. Prepare a checkerboard by pasting squares or rectangles on a paper. Use one color for the rectangles, another for the background. Choose crayons in the same two colors selected for the whole composition, and use the crayon which is the color of the background only on the squares or rectangles and vice versa.

This would be especially effective for a sequence, such as The Beatitudes, The Lord's Prayer, 1 Corinthians 13.

If white background paper is provided, you will of course need a white crayon for each person.

22. There are many ways to structure a course. One way is to give the members the opportunity to indicate which parts of the Bible seem to invite them most strongly to contemplation and study. Make a survey of these choices and plan what can be included in the time span which is available. Arrange the content in sequence and consider which avenues of art response seem best adapted to each piece of subject matter. (See "Steps in Developing a Course," Part 4: Tools for Planning.)

23. At times there may be specific ways in which a leader may offer guidance to members of the group for sharing meaningfully through interim work. Occasionally this might take the form of suggesting assignments.

One way would be to give out file cards with the following instructions written on one side:

Choose a Bible verse: write it on the back of this card.

Find a picture *or* choose an object *or* create a collage which heightens the verse's meaning.

Bring back your card and your "find" next week.

Another way would be to divide the task of telephoning all the members of the class among three or four students. Ask each caller to convey this message: "Next week, for making collages, we will need a large number of squares of paper of all kinds and textures and colors. Bring in with you whatever you like, cut into squares of approximately five or six inches. We'll put it all 'in the pot' and then each can choose what he or she wants to work with."

(Note: The leader or the Media Committee will need to provide a stockpile to assure a sufficient supply and to add variety.)

24. Successfully making a "personellagram" (the term was originated by Ann Larrimore Oden, teenage student) may call for more analysis and overview than the usual art-response, so it might be a good summary approach. This involves acquaintance with a Bible character and can best be done from the vantage point of knowing as much as we can about his background, his life, and his role in the Bible.

A personellagram is an effort to reflect on paper the kind of individual you find this person to be. Areas of the paper may show qualities of character you feel in him: major decisions he made; crises in his life; influences; interests; essentials of background or environment; impact on other people; achievements in realms of the mind, the spirit, and the physical world; strong feelings; responses to God. Each student will create a piece of work which expresses his ideas about the kind of person this character was.

Suppose the group has worked through the story of Moses for several weeks. To help students pull together their ideas for a

personellagram, you might wish to carry out together one or
more of the following suggestions:

Display on the walls of the room all the work that has been
done in response to the readings about Moses.

Outline together on the chalkboard major events in his life.

List together influences on his development as a person.

Arrange on the Saturation Sally table an assortment of resources for browsing: books with markers inserted at
significant points; copies of great art; poetry; realia; items
or pictures which contribute to an understanding of his
life situation — the times and places in which he lived.

As the group shares the moment of silence before the record
player is turned on and they begin to be exposed to the materials which have been placed out for their absorption, make
clear that we have a change of pace here, and each person indi-
vidually may go and begin working on his personellagram whenever he feels ready to do so.

Make a choice of significant verses out of the readings from
the life of Moses which have been used in previous weeks.
Provide a background of music as the students work and against
this read in sequence, with substantial intervals between, the
verses you have selected.

25. Consider at times offering a choice of papers on which
students may work, instead of providing uniform paper for all.
Varieties of colors, textures, sizes, and prints will allow for individualized preferences.

26. Divide lightweight shelf paper into horizontal strips about
two yards long by six or eight inches wide. Ask each student
to fold his strip into whatever number of paragraphs are to be
read (not over twelve), using the accordion type of fold. Ask
each student to choose one color for his entire response or to
change colors only twice, and that between "frames."

For the Sharing and Analysis, break up into groups of three,
and let each trio share responses with one another. Then pile
the three strips together and fasten with a paper clip so that,
when viewed against the light, each frame shows three responses
superimposed on one another. You will want to test your color
medium ahead of time to be sure that the color is translucent.
Felt-tip markers will probably prove most satisfactory.

27. In preparation for an upcoming session, read daily in your

personal study or devotion time the passages which will be used during the session.

28. Collect scrap materials before and during the course. Secure a set of boxes of uniform size — at least shoe-box size — and label the ends for satisfactory storage. Some of the kinds of materials that may be useful are: papers, fabrics, card or cardboard stock, newspaper, trimmings, wire, toothpicks, stationery supplies, string, thread, yarn, beads, stones, color pages of magazines, scraps of sponge, rags, cotton, cleansing tissues, milk cartons, foil pans, popsicle sticks, plastic containers with lids (cottage cheese cartons), eggshells, jars and cans for paints and water.

29. As the course begins, give the group opportunity to answer, or to begin to think about, this question: "What kind of room would speak to our creativity and our involvement with the Bible?" and then, "What can we do with this room to make it meet our requirements?"

30. A dramatic way to display a series of pieces is on "string-turns." Fasten strings from ceiling to floor in an open space. A rod with rings to which strings can be tied is useful for this. Tape pieces of work which match in size back to back against the string. The "I am's" of the Gospel of John, for example, are effective when displayed in this manner.

31. It will be useful to have portfolios of different sizes for storing work. A portfolio may be made of two pieces of corrugated cardboard of equal size cut from sides of cartons and hinged by a double tape across one length. These can be decorated to suit individual tastes, using wallpaper and wallpaper paste. Dry flat under weights for stiffness and straightness.

32. To intensify effects, an olfactory appeal occasionally may be added to an experience through introducing an appropriate fragrance. Incense, candles, space sprays, or natural greens may be used judiciously with attention to the content of the text and the setting it suggests.

33. A smaller group may work simultaneously on a mural of shelf or project paper. In a larger group there are occasions when individual work may be arranged on a mural and a legend written to accompany the finished work.

34. Tissue paper overlay offers fascinating possibilities for a composite of responses to a passage. This is essentially a collage-

type process in which forms will be cut in response to the reading of the text. When the reading is complete, forms are applied to white drawing paper prepared by brushing with a coat of liquid starch. Tissue is overlapped to create different values, hues, and shades. Before introducing this process, read the instructions carefully, experiment by yourself, and then demonstrate.

At the following session, when overlays are completely dry, the passage may be reread while the students add accents with black ink or paint.

35. A tape recorder may provide an enriched experience for participants in an art-response course. For the study of one passage, such as a psalm, John 15, 1 Corinthians 15:35-58, or Luke 22:14-30, record the passage several times, each time read by a different voice, choosing readers whose voices are contrasting in quality, pitch, and style of use. With this tape at hand you can provide a listen-and-listen-again kind of experience for your students. It is useful to leave spaces between readings on a tape and to make an accompanying sound-signal key to enable you to locate the beginning of each section. This can be done by including between readings gentle strokes on a triangle, differing in number, and making a written memo for reference.

36. There may be times when a special tape could be made up to provide sounds appropriate to a specific passage. If you have a tape hobbyist or an individual who is especially interested in sound effects, such a person might be involved with you in planning for sessions from time to time. He need not be a continuing member of the group, but could be any resource person you can discover in your community. Ask him to read passages several weeks in advance to see what ideas he can suggest to enrich the impressions and experiences of group participants. Such planning might result in a listening experience as background for Bible reading or for a few minutes of meditation at the beginning or end of a session, or could be designed for use during the Saturation Sally period.

37. Work of one thickness (not a collage, unless it be of tissue paper) on medium- or lightweight paper, in which translucent color has been used, may become "transparencies" or "stained-glass windows" after the application of cooking oil. Place the

piece of work face down against plain newsprint or paper towels and dampen gently with oil, applying with a piece of cotton moistened lightly. Wipe off excess oil, and when dry, fasten in a window or an area lighted from behind.

38. For some passages a read-and-reread technique gives opportunity for students to make new discoveries and to respond more satisfyingly. This calls for a planned approach in presenting the biblical material, which should consist of not more than fifteen verses. An example would be Ephesians 4:1-7:

> On the first reading, students may cut forms representing major ideas (see *schnitzen,* page 26).
> On the second reading, each student arranges his forms on a background.
> An interval of silence follows for pasting and meditating.
> On the third reading, sponge printing is applied to background to add texture.

A second example would be the use of James 1:

> The first reading is done while students, with pencils and papers ready, record in order a set of nouns from each paragraph that impresses them, as,
> joy — faith — steadfastness
> wisdom — faith — wave-of-the-sea — wind
> lowly brother — flower — grass
> trial — crown — desire
> gift — lights — shadow
> face — mirror — law — liberty
> tongue — heart
> Reread while each student circles the noun in each paragraph (set of words) which best carries for him the idea of the paragraph.
> Give each student seven circles; on each he is to print one of the words he has selected.
> There is an interval for meditating and pasting these seven circles to a background.
> On the third and last reading, be deliberate, allowing time for each student to record (with paint, felt-tip marker, or crayon) in the area around each word some thoughts which that paragraph suggests to him.

39. Texture may be added to a piece of work by gluing toothpicks, straw, or wadded or finely cut-up paper to what has been recorded by students in response to hearing a Bible reading. Provide time for this process by rereading the same material to deepen thoughts, or by using music to carry further the mood of the passage.

40. Give added texture to work by preparing papers ahead of time to receive recorded ideas. This may be done as persons arrive or may be done on a first reading. Using tempera, surfaces may be printed with sponge or chipboard. Then listeners may respond to the reading of the selected Scriptures for the session, using brush painting, felt-tip marker, crayon, chalk, or schnitzen.

41. Try the art-response method in family groups; it is ideal for use with assorted ages. Gather around a table, or use Masonite boards to which paper is clipped, and let each member of the family choose his spot to work. (This is suited for outdoor or indoor use, at home or away, picnicking, traveling, vacationing, camping, a single session or a series.) The family could choose one book of the Bible for a series, or different members of the family could each have a turn to suggest a passage or story that particularly interests him.

Follow the basic sequence suggested at the beginning of Part 2: Projecting a Session, even for a family experience — getting things together; prayer and a quiet listening-thinking-looking time; reading and response; sharing, prayer.

42. Have a Suggestion Box to encourage expression of any ideas which might be forthcoming from the group. Even *one idea* which without a Suggestion Box could be missed might contribute something BIG to the group's experience. A student may prepare the box with fluorescent-paint designs.

43. Hang or drape netting for a display of objects, pictures, or pieces which have been created in response to listening to the Bible.

44. Basically God is an artist: he uses any material at hand to record his thoughts for us to see and feel. These may be recorded in motion; in light and shadow; in forms that stand firmly or that shimmer, bend, or flow; a fragment of sunlight sifting through a crack to form a one-yard by two-inch shaft of morning brightness patterned on the wall by moving leaves;

drifting wisps of fog or smoke; stones and shells lying on a beach. . . .

45. Transfer some of the most effective results of the group's experience to banners (paper tablecloths and branches picked up in the woods will serve here) or to tissue paper or oiled-paper transparencies for plain windows in the church building (attach these with transparent tape for a temporary placement).

46. To introduce the art-response method:

Have a "Dimensions Party" in a home and share the basic ideas and excerpts from this book.

Have an all-day workshop for an assortment of persons with varied interests and backgrounds — churchwide, community-wide, or for a "family of churches."

Encourage the curriculum or education committee to invest one to three hours in exploring the new approach and setting up an experimental venture.

Arrange a "teaching station" to provide resources and to illustrate the processes.

Use the method in a traditional setting as a fresh approach for part of a session. (See #50.)

Use the approach for a "regular meeting time" with a "regular group" or organization as a "program." We can promise it won't be regular; it will be exciting!

Introduction should include *sampling* the experience as well as talking about it.

47. Use suspended objects for display, especially for the Saturation Sally.

48. Do not overlook corrugated paper of different colors which can be obtained in rolls several inches wide and can be shaped with scissors.

49. Paper sculpture has interesting possibilities. Some persons have created innovative forms in three-dimensional effects when working with collages or mobiles.

50. Make use of the art-response method of teaching-learning as a part of whatever curriculum materials are used in your church:

Read session plans as usual as you prepare for meeting a group. Jot down references to biblical material.

Look up the references in your Bible and read them meditatively, noting the context.

In the margin of your teaching manual, mark with a plus sign the suggestions which seem to you to have the most value for achieving the objectives of the session with your particular group. Use a minus sign for those which seem of less value.

Choose the art medium you think might be effective for response to the suggested Scripture.

Arrange the suggested procedures and activities you have marked + in tentative sequence, allowing a minimum of twenty minutes for using the art-response method with biblical material suggested for the session. Keep in mind the session sequence suggested earlier, providing from regular session plans some elements of worship and some enrichment experience before the reading and art response, and concluding with opportunity to discuss and look at work that has been done, and to pray.

Following this basic outline, any session containing biblical material can be adapted to include a block of experience in art response. If no biblical material is suggested, you might ask your minister or some other knowledgeable person to suggest an appropriate passage that could correlate with the theme and would be meaningful to the age level of the group.

51. Tape as you read the passage the first time during the session and play this back for a reread.

52. Taped music serves certain purposes unusually well in the art-response method of teaching-learning. In planning music for a session, consider that with tapes:

Identifying a certain section or fragment from the index counter is easy.

Providing a listening experience of the desired length with a start-play-finish sequence is possible.

Warming-up time, required by many record players, is not needed, so starting, stopping, and starting again can be managed with less awkwardness.

Recordings not available on records can be included for the session.

53. When a group has become established in the procedures and purposes of the art-response experience, further innovations may be introduced without making the experience less effective. It is still important to keep the responses spontaneous and con-

tinuous and to avoid the pitfall of becoming involved in techniques during the reading. The leader will know when any of the following ideas could be introduced with benefit:

String and glue on paper or cardboard may lend itself to meaningful response.

Yarn stitchery on burlap works out well.

When an appropriate occasion presents itself, try group reading with and without music, in different tempos, humdrum fashion and then with feeling.

Select one passage and offer a choice of several familiar media. Let members of the group respond in whatever medium each one chooses, all working simultaneously as usual.

Cut-tear-and-paste is an interesting variation of schnitzen. The use of fabric is another variation, but good scissors are required.

54. Quotes from *Art Guide: let's make a picture:*[1]

"A child can excel not in trying to do something better than the next child, but in developing his own unique way of expressing what he sees." (page 5)

"The child's creative experiences occur when he utilizes not only what he has been taught, but also what he has discovered." (page 21)

These statements are applicable to the youth or adult as well as to the child.

55. When you can find a poem or a song with lyrics which illuminate the biblical meanings, it might be valid to use such a piece after a reread when you are providing more time to finish last steps, as, for example, while pasting is being completed after a series of cut paper pieces have been produced. In a session with the story of creation, for example, truly enriching would be reading the words "The Creation" written by James Weldon Johnson in *God's Trombones* (Viking Press, 1927).

56. Try the effect known as "scumbling." On occasion persons may wish to soften or blend the total effect of their work to create a mood which they have felt in the Bible passage. This may be done by adding a thin coat of color over the whole piece

---

[1] Published by Association for Childhood Education International, 1969. Originally published by Department of Education, San Diego County, California. Used by permission.

74

when it is finished. By turning chalk on its side, color may be applied over a painted or felt-tip marker work, or a pale color wash may be applied to pencil work or schnitzen, using water color or tempera.

57. For end-of-the-course sharing of discoveries, each person may decorate the outside of a box, using cut-paper designs, paint, or whatever medium appeals to him. Inside he may place a paper on which he has written a statement sharing any discovery he has made during his art-response experience. This should be one he considers to be most exciting or meaningful. Boxes may be lightly sealed with tape, exchanged with another person, and opened and read against a background of music.

All boxes could then be arranged in a three-dimensional setting for a celebration of worship moments.

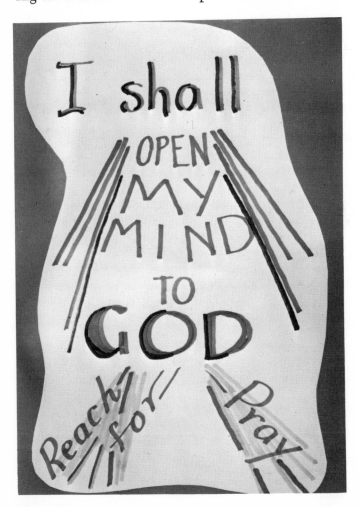

Part 4
TOOLS FOR PLANNING

While the art-response experience may be applied to any part of any curriculum which has biblical content and may deepen and personalize learnings even though applied in a single event, its effectiveness gains momentum when an entire course is built around this approach to the Bible.

A course may be structured beginning from any one of many different starting points:

the interests expressed by a group

the study of a particular book

focus on an historical period

character studies

a doctrinal focus

social or ethical problems

The first step is always to determine what passages in the Bible will be included for the period of time that is projected, allowing for flexibility in pacing the studies. Goals and disciplines need to be established (see Introduction).

Full awareness of the dimensions basic to the approach needs to be developed (Part 1: Considering Dimensions).

Provide a folder or notebook for gathering ideas.

Look carefully at each of the five parts proposed for sequence in a session (Part 2: Projecting a Session) and make notes as you study details. Close acquaintance with this section will help to free you for your own planning.

Begin to gather resources and materials. To assist you in this part of your planning, you will find suggested listings as follows:

Biblical Dimension Reading List — page 77

Bible Background and Enrichment Resource Suggestions — page 78

Art Dimension Reading and Reference List — page 79

Dimensions in Personal Growth Reading List — page 80
Suggested Appropriate Music Recordings — page 81
Art Materials and Recipes — pages 83-85
Addresses of Suppliers (Art Materials, Books, Records) —
page 86

As you move toward projecting your thoughts into the actualization of the experience, you will visualize the group together with yourself as teachers and learners experiencing events in the setting of the space which is to be used. To help at this stage of planning we offer:

The role of the leader — page 87

Profiles in participation, a beginning in getting to know members of the group — page 87

As you move through the course and after its completion, evaluating what is happening and what has happened will be important. Pages 89-90 should be helpful here.

For reference there is also a Glossary of Terms — page 91.

BIBLIOGRAPHY

The New English Bible. New York: Oxford University Press and Cambridge University Press, 1961.

The Bible. Translated by James Moffatt. New York: Harper & Row, Publishers, 1924.

The Holy Bible, Revised Standard Version. Camden, N.J.: Thomas Nelson & Sons, 1952.

Young Readers Bible (RSV). Nashville: Abingdon Press, 1965.

The New Testament from 26 Translations, Ed. Curtis Vaughan. Grand Rapids, Mich.: Zondervan Publishing House, 1967.

The New Testament in Four Versions (King James; Revised Standard; Phillips' Modern English; *New English Bible*). New York: The Iverson-Ford Associates, 1963.

The New Testament in Modern English. Translated by J. B. Phillips. New York: The Macmillan Company, 1958.

Good News for Modern Man. Translated by Robert G. Bratcher. New York: American Bible Society, 1966.

The New Testament, Gospels and the Acts of the Apostles, vol. 1. Translated by William Barclay. New York: William Collins Sons & Co. Ltd., 1968.

The New Testament. Translated by Edgar J. Goodspeed. Chicago: The University of Chicago Press, 1948.

Complete Concordance (Revised Standard Version). Camden, N.J.: Thomas Nelson & Sons, 1957.

Oxford Concise Concordance, Revised Standard Version. Compiled by Bruce M. and Isobel M. Metzer. New York: Oxford University Press, Inc., 1962.

Bible Guides (in 22 volumes). London: Lutterworth Press, and Nashville: Abingdon Press, 1962.

Bible Society Record (Monthly magazine publication). New York: American Bible Society.

Bouquet, Alan Coates, *Everyday Life in New Testament Times.* New York: Charles Scribner's Sons, 1953.

Boyd, James P., *Boyd's Bible Dictionary.* Philadelphia: A. J. Holman Company, 1959.

Eichholz, Georg, *Landscapes of the Bible.* Translated by John W. Doberstein. New York: Harper & Row, Publishers, 1963.

Hamilton, Edith, *Spokesmen for God.* New York: W. W. Norton & Company, Inc., 1949.

Jones, Mary Alice, *Know Your Bible.* Chicago: Rand McNally & Co., 1965.

Keyes, Nelson Beecher, *Story of the Bible World.* Maplewood, N.J.: C. S. Hammond & Co., Inc., 1959.

Lovejoy, Bahija, *Other Bible Lands.* Nashville: Abingdon Press, 1961.

Miller, Madeleine S., and Miller, J. Lane, *Harper's Bible Dictionary.* New York: Harper & Row, Publishers, 1962.

——————————, *Encyclopedia of Bible Life.* New York: Harper & Row, Publishers, 1944.

National Geographic Society, *Everyday Life in Bible Times.* Washington, D.C.: National Geographic Society, 1967.

Northcott, William Cecil, *Bible Encyclopedia for Children.* Philadelphia: The Westminster Press, 1964.

Smither, Ethel L., *A Picture Book of Palestine.* Nashville: Abingdon Press, 1947.

Terrien, Samuel, *The Golden Bible Atlas.* New York: Golden Press, Inc., 1957.

Wolcott et al., *Young Readers Dictionary of the Bible.* Nashville: Abingdon Press, 1969.

Wright, George Ernest, *The Westminster Historical Atlas.* Philadelphia: The Westminster Press, 1956.

Youngman, Bernard R., *The Lands and Peoples of the Living Bible.* Edited by Walter Russell Bowie. New York: Hawthorn Books, Inc., 1959.

For articles on Bible lands:

Aramco World Magazine, published bimonthly by the Arabian American Oil Company, 1345 Avenue of the Americas, New York, N.Y. 10019.

The *National Geographic,* monthly publication of National Geographic Society, 17th and M Streets, N.W., Washington, D.C. 20036.

Aller, Doris and Diane L., *Mosaics*. Menlo Park, Calif.: Lane Magazine & Book Co., 1959.

Borton, Helen, *A Picture Has a Special Look*. New York: Abelard-Schuman Limited, 1961.

Carson, Rachel, *The Sense of Wonder*. New York: Harper & Row, Publishers, 1965.

Chase, Alice, *Looking at Art*. New York: Thomas Y. Crowell Company, 1966.

Cole, Natalie R., *Children's Arts from Deep down Inside*. New York: The John Day Company, Inc., 1966.

Dalglish, William A. *et al, Media for Christian Formation*. Dayton, Ohio: George A. Pflaum, Pub., Inc., 1969.

—————————, *Media Two for Christian Education*. Dayton, Ohio: George A. Pflaum, Pub., Inc., 1970.

Daves, Michael, *Young Readers Book of Christian Symbolism*. Nashville: Abingdon Press, 1967.

Department of Education, San Diego, California, *Art Guide: Let's Make a Picture*. Association for Childhood Education International, 1969. (Simple, well-illustrated; describes step by step processes; paperback; large print.)

Ellis, Richenda, *Natural Creativity in Children*. Washington, D.C.: Institute for Educational Research, 1968.

Feldman, Edmund B., *Art as Image and Idea*. Englewood Cliffs, N.J.: Prentice-Hall, Inc., 1967.

Gettings, Fred, *The Meaning and Wonder of Art*. New York: Golden Press, Inc., 1964.

Guild, Vera P., *Creative Use of Stitches*. Worcester, Mass.: Davis Publications, Inc., 1964.

Harrell, John and Mary, *Communicating the Gospel Today*. (A multimedia book.) Published privately. Berkeley, California, 1968.

Jurack, Simone, *How Is a Banner*. Chicago: Christian Art Associates, 1970.

Kampmann, Lothar, *Creating with Colored Ink*. New York: Van Nostrand-Reinhold Books, 1968.

—————————, *Creating with Crayons*. New York: Van Nostrand-Reinhold Books, 1968.

—————————, *Creating with Poster Paints*. New York: Van Nostrand-Reinhold Books, 1968.

Kelley, Marjorie, and Roukes, Nickolas, *Let's Make a Mural*. Palo Alto, Calif.: Fearon Publishers, Inc., 1958 (pamphlet).

Lavin, E., and Manning, T., *Discovery in Art*. Paramus, N.J.: Paulist/Newman Press, 1970. Also *Discovery in Sign* (9 posters); *Discovery in Sight* (200 slides).

McAfee, Elizabeth A., "Creative Art and the Church Child," *International Journal of Christian Education* (September-October, 1968).

MacAgy, Douglas and Elizabeth, *Going for a Walk with a Line: A Step in the World of Modern Art*. Garden City, N.Y.: Doubleday & Company, Inc., 1959.

Moman, Jean Mary, *Art: Of Wonder and a World*. Blauvelt, N.Y.: Art Education, 1967.

Spelka, Arnold, *Paint All Kinds of Pictures*. New York: Henry C. Walck, Inc., 1963.

Stolz, Mary, *Say Something*. New York: Harper & Row, Publishers, 1968.

World Council of Christian Education and Sunday School Association, *Away In a Manger* (Pictures painted by boys and girls around the world relating to the Nativity). Camden, N.J.: Thomas Nelson & Sons, 1963.

Wright, Kathryn, *Let the Children Paint* (Book and Filmstrip). New York: The Seabury Press, Inc., 1968.

Yolen, Jane, *See This Little Line?* New York: David McKay Co., Inc., 1963.

Contributor to this bibliography: Patricia White of *Ecumedia*.

READING LIST FOR PERSONAL GROWTH AND CHRISTIAN DEVELOPMENT

Bonhoeffer, Dietrich, *Life Together: A Discussion of Christian Fellowship*. Translated by J. W. Doberstein. New York: Harper & Row, Publishers, 1954.

Boyd, Malcolm, *Are You Running with Me, Jesus?* New York: Holt, Rinehart & Winston, Inc., 1965.

Bruner, Jerome S., *The Process of Education*. Cambridge: Harvard University Press, 1960.

Buber, Martin, *I and Thou*. 2nd ed. New York: Charles Scribner's Sons, 1958.

Burke, Carl, *God Is for Real, Man*. New York: Association Press, 1966.

Cunningham, Ruth, *Understanding Group Behavior of Boys and Girls*. Bureau of Publications, Teachers College, Columbia University, 1951.

Clemmons, Robert S., *Education for Churchmanship*. Nashville: Abingdon Press, 1966.

Cooperative Curriculum Project, *The Church's Educational Ministry: A Curriculum Plan*. St. Louis: Bethany Press, 1965.

De Dietrich, Suzanne, *God's Unfolding Purpose*. Translated by Robert M. Brown. Philadelphia: The Westminster Press, 1960.

Griggs, Donald L., "Learning Through Discovery and Relationships," *Spectrum* (January-February, 1970).

Hill, Dorothy La Croix, *Leading a Group*. Board of Education, The Methodist Church, 1966.

Howe, Reuel L., *Herein Is Love*. Valley Forge: Judson Press, 1961.

―――――――, *Man's Need and God's Action*. New York: The Seabury Press, Inc., 1953.

―――――――, *The Miracle of Dialogue*. New York: The Seabury Press, Inc., 1963.

Hunter, David R., *Christian Education as Engagement*. New York: The Seabury Press, Inc., 1963.

Laubach, Frank, *Prayer — The Mightiest Force in the World*. Westwood, N.J.: Fleming H. Revell Co., 1946.

Little, Sara, *Learning Together in the Christian Fellowship*. Richmond, Va.; John Knox Press, 1956.

Miller, Keith, *The Taste of New Wine*. Waco, Texas: Word Books, 1965.

Miller, Samuel H., *Prayers for Daily Use*. New York: Harper & Row, Publishers, 1957.

Minor, Harold D., *New Ways for a New Day*. Nashville: Abingdon Press, 1965.

Niles, Daniel T., *Youth Asks, What's Life For?* Camden, N.J.: Thomas Nelson & Sons, 1968.

Prescott, Daniel A., *The Child in the Educative Process*, New York: McGraw-Hill Book Company, 1957.

Raines, Robert A., *Reshaping the Christian Life*. New York: Harper & Row, Publishers, 1964.

Savary, Louis M., ed., *Listen to Love*. Hicksville, N.Y.: Regina Press, 1969.

Sherrill, Lewis Joseph, *The Struggle of the Soul*. New York: The Macmillan Company, 1957.

Shoemaker, Sam, *Extraordinary Living for Ordinary Men*. Grand Rapids: Zondervan Publishing House, 1965.

Snyder, Ross, *Young People and Their Culture*. Nashville: Abingdon Press, 1969.

Strunk, Orlo, Jr., *Youth Ministry Today*. Nashville: The Methodist Publishing House, Graded Press, 1970.

Suter, John Wallace, ed., *Prayers for a New World*. New York: Charles Scribner's Sons, 1964.

Tournier, Paul, *The Meaning of Persons*. New York: Harper & Row, Publishers, 1957.

――――――――, *The Whole Person in a Broken World*. Translated by John and Helen Doberstein. New York: Harper & Row, Publishers, 1964.

Wilkerson, David, *Hey, Preach: You're Comin' Through*. Westwood, N.J.: Fleming H. Revell Co., 1968.

Wilkinson, Frances, *Growing Up in Christ*. New York: The Seabury Press, Inc., 1960.

Wittenberg, Rudolph, *So You Want to Help People*. New York: Association Press, 1947.

Contributors to this bibliography: William G. Cook, Jr.; Norma Mengel; W. Edward Neighoff; Katherine Smith.

ANCIENT OR EARLY MUSIC

Music played on: a recorder, simple stringed instruments, lute, pipes, oriental or African instruments, harpsichord.

Dunstable, John: *Motets*. Archive Production, Deutsche Grammophon Gesellschaft.

Okeghem, Johannes: *5 Chansons*. Also Archive Production.

[1] Acknowledgments for this section: Virginia Kent Russell, Barbara E. Calkins, and Jenny Smith.

NATURE SOUNDS

Recordings of birds' songs; wind; water, waves, ocean; storms, rain, hail, thunder.

CLASSICAL

This list is almost endless; here are but a few examples to offer an idea of what may be effective:

Bach: *Brandenburg Concerti* (6) mainly strings; one has two flutes and a solo violin in addition to the string orchestra: "Sheep May Safely Graze"; "Jesu, Joy of Man's Desiring," done instrumentally without vocal parts; organ music

Brahms: *Requiem,* Prelude: "How Lovely Is Thy Dwelling Place"

Debussy: *Afternoon of a Faun* (ethereal); *Daphnus and Chloe*

Handel: Any section of the *Water Music; Messiah* (pastorale, overture, selected arias or choruses when the content would contribute to the passages to be read)

Mendelssohn: Any string quartets

Musorgski: *Pictures at an Exhibition,* at least eight pieces, each very descriptive; should be listened to and could tie in with the art idea

Schubert: String quartets

Tchaikovsky: Any of the six symphonies, second movement. The first and last movements would be too exciting and demand the listener's whole attention

MODERN

Again only a few titles are offered, merely to suggest what may contribute to the purposes of the art-response experience:

Afonsky, Nicholas (Conductor): *Masterpieces of Russian Church Music* (Music Guild)

Brubeck, Dave: *The Light in the Wilderness* (Decca), selected portions

Dupré, Marcel: (Widor and Dupré music) *Organ Recital* (Mercury)

Haieff, Alexei: *Concerto for Piano and Orchestra,* Symphony No. 1 (American)

Ives, Charles: *Symphony No. 4* (Columbia)

Kodaly, Zoltan: "Te Deum" (Artia); "Psalmus Hungaricus" (Artia)

Mahler, Gustav: *Symphony No. 2 in C Minor*, "Resurrection" (Columbia)

CURRENT

A list suggested by a college freshman.
The Who (Decca)
The Band (Capitol)
Judy Collins (Electra)

Art materials you may find useful:

Adhesives

White glue
Paste
Liquid starch
Rubber cement
Glue

From the kitchen

Clothespins
Cooking oil
Cornstarch
Eggshells
Flour
Lentils
Paper towels
Plastic containers
Salt
Split peas
Sponges
Toothpicks
Vegetable coloring
Clean containers of glass or metal, empty

Media

Brushes of various types
Chalk
Clay

Crayons
Felt-tip marker
Finger paints
Inks
Pencils
Pipe cleaners
Scissors
Tempera (poster) paint
Water colors

Papers which can be utilized

Bogus paper
Building paper
Cardboard
Construction paper
Classified ad sections of newspapers
Finger-paint paper
Manila
Newsprint
Onion skin
Poster paper
Project paper
Shelf paper
Tissue paper
Typing or mimeograph paper
Wallpaper

ART MATERIALS

83

Scrap Materials

Wire scraps, including telephone wire
Boxes of all types, sizes, and shapes
Round containers
Plastic bags
Jars
Popsicle sticks
Styrofoam
Clothes hangers
Empty sewing-thread spools
Empty bolts from fabric and edgings
Scrap minutia from notion departments
Buttons
Braids and edgings
Tape
Scraps of fabric or thread
Masonite
Wood
Enamel paint
Wallpaper books
Paint chips (from hardware store)
Magazines
Newspapers
Clean paper scraps of any kind
Sawdust
Sand
Pebbles, stones
Scrap jewelry
Rags for cleanup

Stationery

Clips
Pins
Posterboard
Rulers
Thumbtacks

Storage Notes

Store brushes clean, bristle ends up, standing in jars
Box scrap materials according to type; in stacks; label ends or cut them out for easy access
Store papers flat with dividers of light cardboard or contrasting sheets between
Use large portfolios made of scrap sheets of corrugated cardboard and hinged with tape at one edge for large materials or finished work to be protected
Always cover all paints and pastes tightly when not in use

CLAY 1

1 cup salt
½ cup cornstarch
½ cup boiling water
Mix salt and cornstarch
Add water and stir thoroughly

Knead well when cool.

Put mixture in refrigerator in plastic bag.

>This clay can be painted when dry or you can add the color to the water at the start.

CLAY 2

1 cup water
1 cup salt
1 teaspoon powdered alum
½ cup water

>Mix well. Store in covered jar or bag in cool place.

CLAY 3

3 cups flour (or part cornstarch)
2 cups salt
2 tablespoons corn oil or vegetable oil
1½ cups water

>Keep in plastic bag in covered can till ready to use.

CLAY DOUGH 4 (Needs no refrigeration)

1½ cups water and
½ cup salt

>Bring to boil, then remove from heat. Add:

1 tablespoon oil
1 teaspoon alum
food coloring if desired

>Quickly mix in

2 cups flour

>Knead to easily handled consistency.

FINGER PAINT

½ cup lump starch softened in cold water
1 pint of boiling water

>Add boiling water to starch, stirring till clear. When cool, add:

½ cup mild soap flakes
¼ cup talcum powder

>Add poster paint or food color. Stir well. Put into covered jars.

Denominational mail order houses

Local art suppliers

Newspaper printers (newsprint)

Notion and housewares departments (scrap boxes and other scrap materials)

Paper hangers (scrap rolls and sample books)

School supply stores; hobby shops

Members of the group

The congregation (place a notice in the church bulletin or parish paper listing materials which are useful; then provide an attractive receptacle to receive them)

Your church library and public library

American Bible Society
1965 Broadway
New York, New York 10023

Mass Media Ministries
2116 North Charles Street
Baltimore, Maryland 21218
    (Bi-weekly newsletter)

Christian Art Associates
1801 West Greenleaf Avenue
Chicago, Illinois 60626

Full Circle Associates, Inc.
218 East 72nd Street
New York, New York 10021
    (Posters)

Argus Communications
3505 North Ashland Avenue
Chicago, Illinois 60657
    (Posters)

To learn as well as teach

To communicate the framework of the experience, establishing
guidelines

To create settings

To make plans for and set the tone for Opening the Heart to God

To establish the Disciplines

To know the persons and invite each to involvement

To be familiar with the learning tasks in which members of the
group may be engaged

To arrange for the hearing, seeing, and touching experiences of
the Saturation Sally

To plan for and prepare the reading of the Bible

To collect and make ready art materials

To bring each session to a close in meaningful worship moments

To arrange for cleanup and storage

To evaluate sessions and to project coming ones

To obtain resources and resource persons

To encourage openness to God and to one another

In planning a survey to determine the interests, needs, and ideas of persons who will be engaging together in an art-response experience, you may want to include some of the questions below, or they may suggest areas you would like to explore. Members of the teaching team and any member of the course you might wish to include could serve as a committee to develop a "Profiles in Participation" form to be distributed at the first session and completed in five or ten minutes. The responses will be very helpful in planning the sessions to follow. Further clues for direction will come from your own observation of session-to-session responses and expressions of need. See pages 89-90, Evaluation, for specific suggestions.

A Suggested Form:

1. List passages, books, or stories in the Bible which especially intrigue you or spark your questions.

2. What are your hobbies/ major interests?

3. What are your career leanings?

4. Have you religious problems or questions which you can state? __Yes
__No
If "yes," please write here anything you wish. We hope you will find some opportunities to discover answers for yourself through the group's art-response experience.

5. Have you art materials at home that you would like to work with in this course?
__Yes If "yes," please specify
__No (chalks, pastels, paints, crayons, tempera paints, clay, paper, brushes, etc.).

6. What are your goals in life, or what do you think is most important?

YOUR NAME: _____
ADDRESS: _____
TELEPHONE: _____
GRADE: (If under 18)_____
SCHOOL: _____
CLUBS OR ORGANIZATIONS
IN WHICH YOU PARTICIPATE: _____

In order to move most effectively toward the goals you have set, you should survey your progress toward them, take a reading of where you are and how far you have come, and make a correction to keep the ship on course if that is needed.

This evaluation should be done continuously, periodically, and always at the conclusion of the course.

CONTINUOUS EVALUATION: Suggestions for Session-by-Session Analysis

What would have made the session more effective? Made it move more smoothly? Involved persons more completely? Utilized space more advantageously?

What can I learn from the things students said and did?

Am I spending adequate time digging deep enough in my involvement with the Scriptures ahead of time?

Think of specific persons in the group. What evidences can I see of their life situations and issues? How can I utilize their skills? Their *being?*

Write a specific goal before the session as you plan, and afterward ask yourself as you reread it: "Did I move toward this goal?"

PERIODIC EVALUATION: Questions to Think About

In what ways has each student become involved? Write down specific persons, their specific involvements.

How have resources persons been used? Who else would have a skill or a contribution to make to our group experience? Are there resource persons who have been overlooked? Art materials which are being missed?

Are there goals clearly in focus for the group? Do I ask, "What are their goals, not, what are my goals?" Have the group members developed goals of their own?

Work to establish a mood of openness so persons will feel free in the expression of their ideas for structuring the experience and adding to its meaning. This is more than reminding them of a "Suggestion Box" where they can deposit a thought; it requires being available to ask the right question of the right person at the right time. It is truly hearing and seeing the members of the group because you care about each one. It is asking God to let his love come through you to PERSONS and to let your love get through to them.

Write out your thoughts about the shared experience, using the following headings:

Problems I have had, or others have had

Recommended improvements

Satisfactions we have experienced, high moments

Ideas to carry out

Follow up

Give others an opportunity to evaluate, too. One student, given this opportunity, wrote:

I have learned very much during this course. It was different; that is probably why I liked it so much. I felt I could just open my heart and give everything within it to whatever I was doing.

New ideas often call for new vocabulary, as witness the concepts wrapped up in the new words that have been evolved to meet the demands of the exploration in space.

Some of the terms below are well established in the process of education: others will be found completely new in usage as they apply to this art-response teaching method. Still others — a very few — have been coined to meet a communications need associated with a new experience.

art-response experience An event or a series of events in which a listener responds nonverbally and with continuous use of art materials while the Bible is being read; in a wider sense, the totality of which such events form the center.

collage A work of art resulting from arranging and attaching assorted pieces of material to a background.

crossing point A juncture at which the learner becomes aware of some meaning of the gospel for his own life and appropriates that meaning or a part of it.

curriculum The sum of all learning experiences resulting from a teaching-learning situation designed to carry out the church's objective.

dimension A concept involving a multitude of points moving through space to create a magnitude or body.

droodles The felt-tip marker work resulting from a more or less automatic scribble, outline, or design produced while the person is absorbed in listening to the reading of the Bible.

gospel God's continuous redemptive action toward man, known especially in Jesus Christ.[2]

learning tasks Phases in the process of his own growth in which the learner may become actively engaged.

media That through which a force acts to transmit an effect, as, in art media, the material with which a person creates a concrete form of his idea.

monochrome A painting, drawing, or work in a single color or hue.

objective The ultimate end or purpose which is sought for fulfillment.

organizing principle The rationale for including and arranging elements of the curriculum.

personellagram An art piece representing with forms the elements which make up the totality of one particular person — his qualities, drives, skills, characteristics, attitudes, personality, interests, achievements, frustrations, and experiences.

[2] *The Church's Educational Ministry,* section 818.

potential for being The latent possibilities which exist in one individual and could become realized as part of his total person.

realia Real objects which can be included for observation or study.

sampling session A preliminary event in which a brief experience is offered to demonstrate or suggest what may be to come.

Saturation Sally A nonverbal block of activity which includes opportunity to explore, against a background of music, a display of visual materials designed to create a mood and stimulate thinking and feeling.

schnitzen Freehand cutting and pasting.

self-picture An individual's concept or total idea of what he himself is.

translucencies Pieces of art work through which light can be seen but through which objects cannot be clearly distinguished.

For fuller understandings of the meanings of these terms see the index to enable you to locate them in context.

ADDENDUM

Meeting

As my ears hear, my mind leaps up,
My heart is stirred to fire;
My fingers shape the thoughts that flow.
I reach for God with live desire. . . .
   In color, texture, line, and form
   My bird glides out amid the storm
   And finds a branch to rest and stay
   Along his wide and winter way.
So I record this moment known
That lifts me up while I am still.
In beauty I respond to God . . .
May I fly forth to do his will. . . .

                 L.H.Y.

INDEX

94